A WINDOW TO THE PAST - A VIEW TO THE FUTURE

A GUIDE TO PHOTODOCUMENTING HISTORIC PLACES

By
Frederic J. Athearn

Foreword By
Gregory D. Kendrick

Photography By
Frederic J. Athearn

Bureau of Land Management
Colorado State Office
Denver, Colorado
1990

Cover Photograph: Boarding House at the San Juan Chief Mill, Mineral Point, Colorado.

Series Production: Frederic J. Athearn

PREFACE

This volume represents a new work in Colorado's popular Cultural Resources Series. We have published numerous volumes about archaeology and history, but few of them provide information about historic preservation techniques. This volume is based on many years of the author's personal experience, in the preparation of formal documentation for historic sites. Much of the information in this study is about the development of alternative types of archival recordation begun by the Bureau of Land Management in Colorado, and that is now accepted practice in various states.

I hope this document serves as a practical guide to photodocumenting historic (and prehistoric) properties whether they are in a rural setting, as most BLM sites are, or whether they are strictly urban oriented. In either case, preserving our past so that future generations can have a graphic knowledge of our legacy is vitally important.

I am pleased to present this work to both the professional reader as well as to the general public. I am confident that everyone will gain some new ideas from this volume which also represents the 30th Cultural Resources Series book. We started publishing these monographs in 1976 and I am pleased to note that this series has become a well-regarded part of the body of literature over the years.

H. Robert Moore
State Director
Colorado

TABLE OF CONTENTS

FOREWORD

Photography is not commonly equated with historic preservation. Yet, one of my first responsibilities as architectural historian with the Wyoming State Historic Preservation Office involved photographing sites along the historic Overland Stage Route. I recall vividly lurching from one trail rut to another as our four-wheel drive vehicle followed the old stage corridor through southern Wyoming. Time, weather, and frenetic oil and gas activity have taken their toll of the trail's historic resources since I visited the route in 1979. Today, the large format, black and white photographs that we produced of the old stone stage stations constitute an irreplaceable visual record of their existence. Physical preservation may not have been feasible, but at least a photographic record of their appearance has been preserved for posterity.

The National Park Service has long recognized the importance of archival quality, large format photography as an important historic preservation tool. Since the formation of the Historic American Buildings Survey (HABS) in 1933, photographic documentation has played an active and varied role in its preservation programs. The HABS collection now contains more than 130,000 photographs depicting an incredibly diverse cross-section of our nation's architectural heritage. Preservationists, authors, historians, genealogists, architects, and students are but a few of the researchers who have discovered the usefulness of the collection.

Individuals and local, state, and Federal agencies will find this volume a valuable preservation manual. The publication is divided into four main parts and includes a useful bibliography. The text is also supplemented with a portfolio which contains examples of HABS quality photography and measured drawings. Collectively, the individual chapters not only outline a pragmatic methodology for taking pictures but also point out problems commonly associated with archival processing. *A Window to the Past--A View to the Future* will prove a useful guide for people wishing to preserve historic structures through photography.

Gregory D. Kendrick
Senior Historian
Rocky Mountain Region
National Park Service
Denver, Colorado

Introduction

The use of photography to preserve historic places and sites is not new. Photographers have many times saved the past "accidentally" as they photographed everyday scenes as part of their work. In many cases, people experimenting with the new art of photography made major contributions to historic preservation by virtue of their recording contemporary life around them.

The Flatiron Building, in New York City, was fairly new at the time Edward Steichen took his famous photo of it. The photograph shows us architectural details that were subsequently modified over the years. The photo also illustrates the environment of New York City at the time. Another example of photography giving us a view into the past is Dorthea Lange's wonderful Depression Era work. While Lange was mostly interested in the intense suffering of the people, her photographs show what the buildings, houses, cars, and the environment of the time all looked like. This too was historic preservation by "accident".

During the 1930s, the federal government, established a formal process for recording historic properties. It involved the use of architects, historians and photographers to create permanent records of significant historic buildings in the United States. This project was part of the many artistic efforts undertaken by the Franklin D. Roosevelt administration. There were also writer's projects that produced histories of the states, along with artistic efforts contributing murals and paintings to government buildings. Photographers and architects, too, were commissioned to record historic places. The collections that developed would be permanently stored in the Library of Congress for research, and if needed, restoration and/or reconstruction of historic properties. The program was called the Historic American Buildings Survey and was administered by the National Park Service.

Over the years, thousands of projects have been entered into the Library of Congress's HABS/HAER collections. They represent all kinds of buildings, structures, and features throughout the United States. Many of the HABS records are of major national monuments like the capitol building in Washington, D.C. But, increasingly, locally significant, vernacular historic properties have come to be regarded worthy of preservation.

This volume will explore the proper procedures for producing photographs that should last several hundred years. It also will discuss proper handling techniques for photos and it will provide guidance for the recordation and subsequent preservation, on film, of our historic buildings and places.

PART ONE

THE ARCHIVAL DOCUMENTATION OF

HISTORY

Part I

Archival Documentation of History-An Overview

History, by definition, involves the written record of mankind. That in itself would suggest that documentation is important for both present and future historians. In order to leave something for the future the past must be documented in such a way that the physical evidence will survive more than a few years.

Historic photos still exist because of the quality of the medium used as this 1882 photo shows. Photo: Union Pacific Railroad

Recently, it has become obvious that books and other historic materials that have been generated since the 1850s are in considerable danger of being lost due to acidic paper disintegrating. Libraries throughout the world have undertaken programs to de-acidify documents in order to save them. The Library of Congress has a major program to save books through special treatment programs to remove acids.

Documentation of historic places and events is not just a matter of the written word. Since the mid-nineteenth century, photography has taken an increasingly important place in documenting the past. Photos, luckily, proved to be pretty archivally stable because of various chemical techniques that were applied to processing prints and negatives. While many of the prints and negatives made were subsequently damaged or destroyed by mishandling, a great number of very delicate materials did survive.

Unlike published materials, photographic requirements were such that new technology in paper making could not be used. In the 1880s, paper made of wood pulp became commonly available. Cheap magazines and newspapers used this much less expensive paper to print on. Hence, the term "pulp" magazines came into vogue.

Older paper technology that used linen (or rags) for the paper pulp continued to be used, but due to the cost involved, was only considered appropriate for special documents. Unfortunately, while the cost of paper went down thanks to wood pulp, the material proved to be very acidic and would self-destruct over a period of 50 to 100 years.

Pioneers of Early Photography

Of course, no one knew at the time, that new wooden pulp paper would be so destructible. Luckily, it was not particularly good for photographic print making. Mid-nineteenth century photo technology consisted of taking a sheet of linen based paper with a baryta sub-strate, and coating it with a photosensitive emulsion (usually of albumen). This process, introduced in France in 1850 by Louis-Desire Blanquart-Evrard, used albumen from eggs to hold a solution of silver-nitrate. The image was printed out using sunlight.

If a print were properly fixed, using gold chloride, for instance, the photo was quite permanent. However, if the print was not processed correctly, such as not removing fixer residue or perhaps using water that was contaminated by minerals like iron, prints could yellow, be stained, or fade from existence. The same fate could be suffered by negatives, but often new print could be made from a damaged negative.

The first true photographs were exposed on metal that was sensitized to accept an image. Daguerreotypes, named for their inventor J.M.L. Daguerre, were metal sheets upon a positive silver image was affixed. Daguerreotypes were introduced in 1839 in France. The final product was usually mounted, framed, and placed behind a sheet of glass. There was a good reason for this care. Daguerreotypes were easily scratched and could be damaged through careless handling. There are many example of daguerreotypes still in circulation.

Tintypes, patented in 1856 by Hamilton Smith, were another photographic medium that represented the birth of photography. A thin sheet of iron was used to provide a base for light sensitive material, yielding a positive image. Like daguerreotypes, tintypes were easily scratched and therefore had to be protected with glass and cardboard frames. The cardboard backing, however, was sometimes highly acidic and damaged the tintype image.

Photography advanced when it was discovered that light sensitive materials could be coated on plate glass. The ambrotype, introduced in 1851, became the most popular form of this early glass plate technology. The medium and emulsion could then be placed in a camera and exposed yielding a negative image. The "negative" would then be printed, either through enlarging or contact printing, into a positive image. The glass plate was regarded as a breakthrough because it was easier to use than were the old tintype processes. In addition to being portable, the glass plate could be made in various sizes. It was just a matter of coating the material with emulsion.

F.S. Archer introduced a similar process in 1851 called the collodion process in which a thin layer of liquid collodion carrying bromide salt was placed on a glass plate. The plate was exposed while wet and then developed. The wet-plate processes such as collodion and ambrotype were advances, but still not practical for everyday applications.

Despite the relatively easy process that glass plates represented, they still confronted the amateur photographer with a real challenge. The emulsion had to be coated on the glass in the dark. Then the plate was rushed to the camera before it dried out and it was exposed, often up to five minutes, to get a decent photo. The plate had to be developed right away and properly dried. After all that effort, plates could easily be broken in transport or during printing. In the 1870s dry plates were introduced.

In 1871 R.L. Maddox invented a process that used gelatin as an emulsion. Coated on a glass plate, it provided a very sensitive photo medium that was portable, could be mass produced and was easy to use. The new dry-plate/gelatin system soon replaced the older wet-plate technologies and made mass photography possible. Serious amateurs could now make pictures with relative ease. The use of gelatin as an emulsion has remained the standard for nearly all films to this day.

Nevertheless, glass plates made photography a popular medium. Glass plates allowed for portability, relative ease of use, and they could be preserved for a long time. Matthew Brady, during the Civil War, made thousands of wet glass plates that recorded photographically, for the first time, warfare. During the mid-1870s, William Henry Jackson photographed hundreds of places ranging from Yellowstone National Park to the Mount of the Holy Cross. Most of the photos were as a result of U.S. Geological Survey expeditions under the guidance of Ferdinand V. Hayden. The environment and landscape of the nation became commonly known through publications of Hayden's surveys.

As photography advanced, so too did printing. By the late 1880s it was possible to reproduce photographs on a printing press. This revolutionized the newspaper trade, which began to publish photos of important events and places. Popular interest in photography soared. George Eastman, realizing the potential of the market, invented a new emulsion base that was flexible, unbreakable, and that could be rolled. The material was known as "film" which is exactly what it was. Emulsions could be coated on a thin cellulose nitrate base which made the box camera possible.

It was possible to create photographs in a cheap box camera, send it back to Eastman Kodak where the film would be processed and prints made. The camera would be reloaded with film and returned to the owner. Millions of snapshots were being made. They documented everyday life in America. Not only were important events and places recorded, but little common occurrences were now being preserved on film. Thanks to Eastman's invention, the recording of history on film began on a large scale. Family albums, newspaper photographs, art photography, photo journalism and numerous other types of photography all documented current events.

Despite the availability and ease of use of film, (which also introduced the motion picture industry), the images were still only in black and white. Sometimes toning in brown, sepia, or other colors would add "color" to a photo, but basically it was a black and white/grey image. Many users wanted a color image that would reflect what the human eye could see. Photo technology did not allow for color because of the complexity of film design. One substitute for color was to take a black and white print and have an artist hand color it. This was a very popular medium in the early to mid-twentieth century. Many thousands of hand-colored portraits survive to this day.

But coloring was not the same as an actual "color image". As early as 1915 the German photographic firm of Agfa was experimenting with something they called the "autochrome" process. By dying standard film, it was possible to create a "color" of sorts. The results were a pale [pastel] effect that was not particularly pleasing. It was also very expensive. World War I put an end to these experiments.

In the mid-1930s Eastman Kodak introduced a revolutionary new film. It was based on black and white negative film, but in the processing step, color dyes were added, resulting a realistic color transparency. This was made possible by the invention of color dye couplers which allowed for the basic colors needed to produce a color image. Layers of magenta, cyan and yellow were added to the basic image. This use of three color layers is very similar to the four-color printing process used for magazines and books.

The new film was called Kodachrome (chrome meaning a positive transparency). The film was as significant to photography as was the introduction of flexible film itself. For the first time, color images could be created easily. Prints could be made from them, although the early color printing process was very expensive and difficult. As time went along, new color films were introduced that used the modern technology of dye coupled three layered colors built into the film, not added on to it. Such films as Kodak's Ektachrome, Agfachrome, Fujichrome, Ilfochrome, and all other transparency films use this technology. Kodachrome remains a after-exposure dye process.

As transparency films were created, negative image color films were also invented. Color negatives are based on the same three-layered dye coupled systems as positive films. The difference is that a negative can be printed into a positive image, in color. The process is quite similar to photomechanical reproduction used in offset printing.

In the late 1940s, Dr. Edwin Land invented an instant film process that yielded prints directly from a camera. The Polaroid system used gelatin on paper technology to create a positive image in the camera. This was rather similar to the old tintype process. But the film was processed within the camera using liquid capsules and rollers to spread the developer across the paper. Thus, instant photography was born. As time progressed, Polaroid developed a color print process and later a

Fungus and algae are also damaging to prints and negatives. Dirty trays, processors, and tanks can cause algae or fungus growths that can be transferred to film and paper. The use of clean equipment will prevent the problem. There are also cases when old paper, stored under less than ideal conditions will show algae growth. For this reason, only fresh paper should be used for archival printing.

A recent innovation in papers is the resin coated or "water resistant" paper. The idea behind it is to take normal linen based paper and coat it with a plastic (polyethylene) material, thus making the paper waterproof. An emulsion is coated on the base paper and does not penetrate into the paper stock. The problem with resin coated papers is that the image "rides" on a plastic coating, making it susceptible to loss. Early resin coated papers sometimes had the emulsion literally slide off the paper, losing the entire print.

Because resin coated paper is considered by some to be unstable, the Library of Congress will not accept it for archival quality prints. Only linen fiber base paper is acceptable for a permanent collection. There is considerable debate over the archival qualities of resin coated paper. Eastman Kodak claims that it is every bit as stable as fiber based paper. However, the Library of Congress does not agree and still does not accept resin coated paper.

Unfortunately, virtually all prints that are commercially made today are on resin coated paper. Whether the print is from the corner drug store or a professional laboratory, it is almost certain to be made on resin coated paper. It may not be archivally permanent. However, there are custom processors who will print on fiber base paper and who know how to finish work to archival standards.

Another film medium that is not particularly suitable for archival permanence is color. Color is not archivally stable because it uses organic dyes to make the color image. These organisms deteriorate over a period of time and the print/negative/transparency will disappear from the film or paper base.

Only Kodachrome is known to be long-lasting because of the process that is used to create an image. Kodachrome transparencies that are more than fifty years old still remain in good condition. All other transparency and negative color films have long since faded. Since Kodachrome is only some fifty five years old, we really do not know how long it will last. It is, at present, the most archivally permanent color medium available.

Because color is relatively new, we do not know how long some prints may survive. Older color prints like Kodak Ektacolor have faded in twenty to thirty years. Kodak states that its new materials like resin coated color paper will last as long as black and white. Perhaps this is true if the black and white is printed on resin coated paper. It is not true when fibre base paper is used.

7

Another process, called Cibachrome (Ciba/Geigy), uses metallic dyes to create an image on paper. It is claimed that color prints made by the Cibachrome process (which can only be used with color transparencies), will last for at least 100 years. However, since the process is only thirty 30 years old, no one knows how permanent it really is.

The only certain way to arrest deterioration of color materials is to freeze them. By keeping color films and prints at 0 degrees Fahrenheit, deterioration is stopped indefinitely. However, in most circumstances keeping film and prints frozen is not very practical. In the case of color, the best advice is to keep the medium in a cool, dry, dark place and hope for the best. If there are negatives/transparencies that are very valuable, they should be copied on to archivally permanent black and white media.

Archival Storage

In addition to film and paper, curation of materials is important if they are to last. There are numerous ways to handle films/papers. Equally, there are many methods of restoration and salvage for photographic materials. A number of excellent publications devoted to this subject are available. In particular, Eastman Kodak's *Conservation of Photographs*, (Rochester, New York: Eastman Kodak Company, 1985) is outstanding.

To conserve photos many of the same rules apply to handling the materials. Cool, dark, dry places are best for photographic media. Prints should be stored in acid free envelopes and negatives should be kept in an acid free environment such as envelopes. Polyvinylchoride (PVC) slide/negative holders should NEVER be used because they give off acids and gasses that destroy emulsions. So-called archival plastic holder are better for slides/negatives, but not as good as acid-free envelopes. Slides can be stored in metal boxes so long as they have no plastic slide separators/holders in them. Again, the plastic gives off gasses.

Storage of prints requires cool, dark and dry places. Cardboard, black construction paper, manila envelopes, paper envelopes, non-rag bond paper, print holders such as "magnetic" holders, and albums that use non-acetate plastic are all unacceptable for archival permanence. Paper products that are not acid-free will cause print/negative deterioration as acids and gasses eat away at the photo materials. Albums with cheap plastic in them give off toxic gasses and destroy emulsions. The only sure way to curate for the long-term is to use archival supplies that are specifically designed for museum quality curation.

Conclusions

The preservation of photographic materials is important so that we can leave images of both our past and our present to the future. Planning for the future when recording historic places and building is critical if the record is to last. Old photos need special treatment and need to be handled like rare documents. They are delicate and can easily be damaged. They also are very important in giving us a window on the past.

As we record modern day places for future use, awareness of archival
procedures and the various limitations of films is critical. The wrong film, the wrong paper, or poor processing will severely limit the life of photographic records as will improper finishing. Photographs should be permanent and by adhering to some basic guidelines, and with a little extra effort, a photographer's work can last for hundreds of years.

PART TWO

THE FORMAL DOCUMENTATION OF

HISTORIC PROPERTIES

Part II

Formal Documentation of Historic Properties

Prior to the mid-1930s, there was no national program designed to formally document historic properties. Local and state historical societies may have attempted to record sites and buildings, but there were no standards that provided for long-term preservation of recordation materials. In 1935 the Historic Sites Act was passed. Among the many provisions of this legislation was the establishment of the Historic American Buildings Survey (HABS) to be administered through the U.S. Department of the Interior, National Park Service.

While the HABS was to some extent a "make work" program originally designed to employ architects, and later photographers, it also was very important in establishing national standards for archival recordation. The HABS staff designed a system of formal documentation that would allow for complete and detailed recording of architectural sites that were of historic significance. One of the key provisions of the HABS standards was long-term archival quality for documentation. A HABS collection was established in the Library of Congress to store the records over time. HABS created stringent requirements for historic preservation leading to the first comprehensive efforts at archival documentation.

HABS standards, to be discussed later, were developed in association with the American Institute of Architects (AIA), the National Park Service, the Library of Congress, historians, librarians, archivists, and photographers. A national architectural archive maintains these standards while assuring curation for the records. HABS was expanded in 1969 when the Historic American Engineering Record (HAER) was established. The purpose of HAER was to create records of historic features that were engineered or that represented industrial creations. The HAER recorded things like bridges, dams, railways, factories, and other historic places considered "non-architectural". The standards for HAER are somewhat different than HABS, however the drawing and photographic standards are the same.

Preparing a HABS/HAER is a three part process that involves specific tasks for the authors/architects/photographers. Each part can be accomplished individually, but they all add up to a completed documentation.

Measured Drawings
The first component for HABS (and HAER) documentation is architectural (or engineering drawings). These drawings must be made on HABS/HAER provided mylar because it has certain data sections pre-printed on it. The mylar is also dimensionally stable and archival quality. Special

inks such as Pelikan must be used and the drawings must be prepared to HABS standards for line weight, lettering size, and so forth. HABS drawings can be very complex depending on the size and scope of the building (engineering feature) being recorded. Complete drawing standards are outlined in: *Field Instructions for Measured Drawings*, (Washington, D.C.: National Park Service, n.d.).

Most HABS/HAER measured drawing projects require no less than:

1. Site Plan of area including plants, geographic features, roads, etc.

2. Elevations of all sides of structure

3. Detailed drawings of special features

4. Cross-sections of structure

5. Field notes and photographs

6. Cover sheet with information block

Normally, it requires a professional architect to measure and draw HABS/HAER plans to specification. An architect can provide rough field measured drawings and a draftsman can then complete the final drawings.

Historical Documentation

The next part of a HABS/HAER project involves documentation of the site/feature. Like using an architect to prepare architectural drawings, a professional historian is usually required to properly research and write the historical documentation needed by HABS/HAER. HABS/HAER needs more than just historic use of a site.

Part I of the process requires the historian to research ownership of the property to determine its legal location, to find out when it was built, who the architect was, and who the builder was. In addition to this data, a search for original plans is undertaken and any alterations or additions are noted. The structure/site must also be placed in a historical context. Context means how the property fits into the history and social structure of a given period of time. Context involves the development of a overall picture into which a historic site fits.

Part II of the historical documentation process involves architectural information that includes architectural character, description of the exterior, description of the interior, and descriptions of the site.

Part III of documentation requires the historian to discuss where information was found. This includes architectural [historic] drawings, old photographs of the property, interviews with persons knowledgeable about the site, the creation of a bibliography, and supplemental materials such as deeds, records, etc.

Part IV of the documentary process asks for project information including author, photographer and architect. It also gives information about the project, agency involvement, dates of recordation, and other vital information. All of the data sheets that are created for a HABS/HAER project must be typed on 100% rag bond paper (archival). It is preferred that the documentation be Xeroxed onto bond paper. All attachments, appendices, plans, photocopies, etc. must be xeroxed onto archival paper. Information for complete historical documentation for a HABS/HAER is found in: *Historian's Procedure Manual*, (Washington, D.C.: HABS, National Park Service, 1983).

Archival Photography

The final part of a HABS/HAER project is the photography. In addition to architectural drawings, photos are vital because they give views of what a property looks like. Because photographs must be architectural, HABS/HAER will accept only large format negatives that are corrected for distortion using a view camera. HABS will not accept negatives any less than 4 inches by 5 inches (4 x 5). The preferred format is 5 x 7 inches. Negatives larger than 8 x 10 inches are not acceptable.

A photo shot on 4 x 5 film can yield considerable detail.

The reason for requiring a view camera is that it is the only machine that can be adjusted to compensate for distortion and it can correct perspective problems. Additionally, a large format negative provides a wealth of detail that is often hard to get with smaller format film. Naturally, only black and white film is acceptable due to its archival stability.

HABS/HAER specifies the following equipment and film:

1. Lenses. No "soft focus" (like an Imagon) lenses may be used. The complement of lenses will include at least one normal focal length, one wide angle, and one telephoto lens. They must have adequate covering power to accommodate both front and rear board movements without vignetting.

2. Filters. Photographer's choice. However, the use of a pola screen is encouraged. Also, when shooting wooden structures, brickwork, stonework, and other natural materials, a Medium Yellow filter is very useful in enhancing details. In some cases an Orange filter will help enhance grain and detail more than a Yellow filter will.

3. Film. A fine grain, cut film, with a minimum resolving power of 80 lines per millimeter high contrast range and 30 lines per millimeter low contrast range is acceptable. Films such as Tri-X, T-Max, Plus-X, etc. are suitable. FILM PACKS ARE NOT ACCEPTED. COLOR FILMS, EITHER NEGATIVE OR POSITIVE ARE ABSOLUTELY NOT ACCEPTABLE. For copy work (old photos, etc.) Kodak Professional Copy Film Type 4125, or equivalent, must be used in making continuous tone copy photographs. For copy line drawings, Kodalith, or similar, film must be used. All films must be in date and have a polyester base. When original negatives, especially historic negatives, are to be copied, the use of black and white direct duplicate films are prepared. Kodak Type 4168 is an example of this kind of film.

4. Paper. All documentary photography produced for HABS/HAER MUST be printed on fiber base paper. It should be double weight, glossy, and finished to archival standards. THE USE OF RESIN COATED PAPER IS UNACCEPTABLE.

Photographing Historic Sites for HABS/HAER

The purpose of HABS/HAER photography is to provide a representation of the site so that in case it were destroyed, modified, or otherwise changed, it could be restored to its original condition. Photographs make this possible because they show what the materials are, how the property is constructed, the over-all site setting, and details of architecture that might not be obvious through drawings. In order to get the photographic information needed, the following steps are suggested:

1. Minimum Architectural Features:

   a. Elevation of front facade.

   b. Perspective view (three quarter), front facade and one side.

   c. Perspective view (three quarter), rear and one side.

   d. Detail of front entrance and/or typical window.

   e. General view of site, showing environmental setting, landscaping, relationship to other buildings.

   f. Interior views (as appropriate), including staircases, fireplaces, kitchens, attic construction, machinery, construction details, and other interior details of interest.

   g. Exterior details, one or more. This can include chimney, shutters, construction, ornamentation, etc.

2. Minimum Engineering/Industrial Features:

   a. Machinery/equipment and their spatial arrangements.

   b. Details of machinery.

   c. Power transmission systems (i.e. turbines, etc.).

   d. General views of the structural systems, roof trusses, etc.

   e. In the case of bridges, views from all sides, trusses, portals, decking, beams, abutments, date plates, etc.

Processing HABS/HAER Photographs

In order to produce archivally stable photographs, both negatives and prints must be handled carefully. The primary culprit in film/paper damage is fixer (hypo=sodium thiosulfate) residue. All film/paper must be treated in a hypo clearing bath such as Permawash, or Orbit bath. Films/papers must be washed both before and after the hypo clearing treatment. A two hour wash is strongly recommended to assure removal of all hypo. HABS/HAER does test for residual hypo and will reject those prints/negatives that fail the Kodak Hypo Eliminator Scale. HABS/HAER also states that film and prints developed using automatic processors have repeatedly failed the hypo tests and therefore are NOT CONSIDERED ARCHIVALLY PERMANENT.

Printing HABS/HAER Photographs

The rules for printing HABS/HAER photographs are somewhat different than might be expected. Because the negatives are large format and can easily yield considerable detail, they are contact printed only. Prints should be made on the next largest size of paper (i.e. 4x5" on 5x7" paper) but not larger than 8x10 inches. All edges of the negative must show in the print. This proves that the negative has not been enlarged or "doctored". The prints should be made on double weight glossy paper (fiber base only).

It is important to know that each negative to be submitted MUST have a HABS or HAER number on it. That number is assigned by HABS/HAER and is unique. Each negative must have a this number on it in sequential order, PRIOR to making contact prints. The numbers should be place in the upper right hand corner (in a clear area) outside of the image area using permanent ink such as Pelikan.

Complete information about preparing photographs for HABS/HAER is found in:

Specifications for the Production of Photographs, (Washington, D.C.: HABS/HAER, National Park Service, n.d.).

Transmittal of A Completed HABS/HAER

The final step in a HABS/HAER project is to assemble the constituent parts and prepare them for submission to HABS/HAER. To gather together all of the drawings, historical documentation and photos in one big pile and send them to Washington is not acceptable. The HABS/HAER project must be properly submitted using archival standards of preparation.

Preparing Documentation

When preparing documentation, the following preservation guidelines should be observed:

1. There should be no smoking, eating or drinking near items of a collection. Paperclips, rubber bands, pins or staples are not to be used. Equally cellophane or plastic covers, tapes, and so forth should not be allowed near the submission items.

2. Paper materials should only be prepared on 100% rag bond (archival) paper, including xerox copies of materials. Normal paper (acidic) should never be mixed into the submission.

3. Marking photographs and other material should only be done with a soft lead pencil. Ink migrates and can soak through photographic and/or archival bond paper. Ballpoint pens should NEVER be used for marking photos or papers.

Preparing Photographs

The preparation of photographs for HABS/HAER submission requires the following:

1. Each negative is placed in an individual acid free envelope, which should be the next size up from the negative. For instance 4 x 5" negatives would go in a 5 x 7" envelope. Each envelope must be typed with required information in the upper right hand corner.

2. Each contact print must be placed on aperture cards (supplied by HABS/HAER). Required information (such as the photo number, HABS/HAER number, etc.) is typed in the upper right-hand corner of the card. These cards are archivally stable and are used in the HABS/HAER collection for easy retrieval of the photos.

3. Photographic data sheets describing equipment, films, filters, lenses, etc. should be provided. This information should include the name of the photographer, the date of the photography, speed and exposure data, and other information important to the project.

4. In addition the information sheets, a Photographic Index must be prepared. In it each photograph must be listed with a description of what the view is. For example, CO-62-1, Facing West means that this is a shot of the building facing to the west of HABS number CO (Colorado)-62 (HABS project)-A (building A)-1 (photo number one).

The HABS/HAER number must always be on the negative and the positive photographs. Using drafting ink and a Leroy pen can provide a neat way of marking the negatives. The HABS or HAER number must be placed in a clear area of the negative (the edge of the negative) and not in the image area of the photograph.

Measured Drawings

Measured drawings are transmitted as part of the over-all package. They are prepared on special HABS mylar and contain the HABS/HAER project number, Each sheet has a sequential sheet number on it. Other than not folding or damaging the sheets, no special requirements are needed to transmit them.

Complete transmittal data for HABS/HAER is found in:

John A. Burns (Ed.), *Recording Historic Structures*, Washington, D.C.: American Institute of Architects Press, 1989.

Transmitting Documentation To HABS/HAER/WASO, (Washington, D.C.: National Park Service, 1985).

Manual For Editing HABS/HAER Documentation, (Denver: National Park Service, Rocky Mountain Regional Office, 1986).

Harley J. McKee, *Recording Historic Buildings*, (Washington, D.C.: National Park Service, 1970).

Normally, completed HABS/HAER documentation should be sent to the National Park Service's Regional Office that is responsible for the states in which the project took place. For complete information about preparing a HABS/HAER, inquiries should be addressed to: HABS/HAER, National Park Service, P.O. Box 37127, Washington, D.C. 20013-7127

Conclusions

HABS/HAER projects represent a very formal and complete form of documentation for historic properties. Often, this level of recordation is required to mitigate the loss of a site. Demolition due to project, especially in an urban setting, will demand that a structure be "preserved" on paper and film. Particularly significant historic properties such as those listed in the National Register of Historic Places, or those that are eligible for National Register listing may be appropriately recorded at the HABS/HAER level.

However, not every structure is suitable for HABS/HAER recordation. There are numerous historic sites that are of "lesser" quality that need to be preserved archivally, but for which HABS/HAER recordation may not be appropriate. For instance, sites that are eligible for inclusion in the National Register of Historic Places may require mitigation. But they are not architecturally or aesthetically important or they no longer retain architectural integrity. Does this mean that they should not be archivally preserved? Most certainly not. While the HABS/HAER process is formal and very stringent, there are other ways to record sites that will fully document their significance and architecture, while also creating records that are every bit as archivally permanent as HABS/HAER products.

PART THREE

ALTERNATIVE ARCHIVAL

DOCUMENTATION

Part III

Alternative Archival Documentation

There are numerous historic properties, that while historically significant and architecturally important, do not, require the level of recordation a HABS/HAER provides. Very many sites are smaller, less architecturally attractive, or less significant places. However, the archival documentation of such properties is every bit as important as HABS/HAER projects. Many lesser historic structures and sites may survive because someone recognized that they should be recorded despite their seeming unimportance.

Over the years, an orderly system of recordation involving several "levels" of documentation that are used to record historic properties has developed. These are in addition to the HABS/HAER process. What might be considered "reduced" or "lesser" levels of recordation are as important as formal recording projects because basic site records for historic properties are created.

Level I Documentation

This is the most elementary method for recording historic properties. It involves field location of a site, the recording of that place, photography of the site's features, and a site/location map. This level of recording should be done for any property, regardless of its "significance" or perceived importance. The reason such a record is critical is that it may be the ONLY physical record of a site. In many cases, the only site records available are those of field recordation. This is especially true of sites dating back only 50 and 60 years.

Level I recordation should include, at the least, the following:

1. Site record form(s). This is the basic tool for recording historic properties in the field. The recording may vary from state to state and agency to agency, but the principle is usually the same. The data contained in the site form provides future researchers with certain information such as:

   a. site location (where is the site geographically or legally located)
   b. site type (what kind of site is it; historic, pre-historic, etc.)
   c. site description (what does the site look like)
   d. site ownership (who owns this property)
   e. site map (sketch of site/area using map grid)
   f. site access (how do you get to the site)
   g. site number (varies by state and agency)

24

h. site environment (site setting in its environment)

i. site significance (is this site significant, i.e. National Register)

j. site condition (what is the condition of this site)

k. site documentation (what existing records are there about this place)

l. site photographs

m. site quad map (location of site on U.S.G.S. Quadrangle map)

The basic record provides researchers, and other users, vital information about the site and how it looked at a certain point in time. The photos and maps will show where it is (was) located and how it appeared. This information is basic to virtually ALL sites, regardless of whether they are HABS/HAER documented or are Level I in quality. Ideally, the site record forms will be xeroxed onto 100% rag bond for archival permanence.

In addition to the site forms, Level I recordation requires that a quality map be used to show where the site is located. This means using a U.S. Geological Survey Quadrangle map that gives enough detail to allow for the site (and associated other area) to be seen. Usually, not only is a legal description needed but also a UTM (Universal Transverse Mercator) coordinate is required.

Additionally, photographs of the site are required. This is one area that a Level I recordation often fails to provide for long-range needs. Usually site photos involve the use of a 35mm camera with some kind of color film. This is NOT acceptable for archival permanence. Color films will generally fade within 25-30 years, leaving the site record incomplete. If we are simply lucky, or if a sponsoring agency demands it, black and white photography is sometimes used for photographing basic site records.

However, since the early 1970s, commercial photofinishers have used resin coated papers and machine processing to print black and white negatives. The result is that both the negatives and the prints are probably not archivally stable and will deteriorate over a period of 30 to 50 years. The use of modern processing technology is not going to provide a very long record for sites that were recently photographed.

The common use of 35mm cameras also promotes photofinishing that is not archivally acceptable. Most 35mm films end up at a drug store or a photo shop where machine prints are common. It is both expensive and time-consuming to have archivally stable 35mm negatives and prints made, but if the goal is long term storage and retrieval of these materials, archival quality is mandatory. In the interest of cost and speed, site record photos are not generally being properly finished and therefore will not survive very long.

The 35mm camera is easy and quick to use, but it does not always provide the level of detail and quality that a larger format negative can. Small format films stretch the limits of resolution [resolution is measured by lines per millimeter] and sharpness. Most 35mm single lens reflex cameras have good lenses on them. But when a 35 mm negative is enlarged to 8x 10 inches or 11 x 14 inches, important details can be lost. The larger the format, the less loss of information.

While some 35mm cameras offer special perspective corrections lenses (PC), which can make limited corrections for architectural work, the small film size limits usefulness of the final image. One place where 35mm film is helpful is in a documentation process where color slides (transparencies) are desired. Using Kodachrome film (for archival life), a 35mm slide can give the viewer an idea of the tones and shades of a structure and what the environment looks like in color. However, this is not a good substitute for archivally stable black and white negatives and prints.

Level II Documentation

This level of documentation represents expansion of Level I (basic) recordation but less than Level III (HABS/HAER) recording. Level II is an excellent tool for recording historic structures/sites that may be eligible for inclusion in the National Register of Historic Places, but that are not of sufficient architectural merit to require a formal project like HABS or HAER. Level II documentation provides archival quality documentation for a site without the expense and time-consuming effort of a Level III. Level II recordation involves three components. They are similar to a HABS/HAER project.

Site Records and Historical Documentation

Since every site should have a record form for it, the basic information may be available without further work. In the case of sites that have no records, a Level I recordation should be prepared. In addition to Level I information, the site will need to have some basic research done on it. In addition to physical characteristics and legal description, a Level II recordation requires prior ownership information, architectural data, and a historic context similar to what is needed for HABS/HAER documentation. However, there is no defined format for this data and it can be prepared in nearly any form desired, so long as the final document is completed on archival bond paper. The guidelines provided in Chapter II for HABS/HAER documentation generally apply to a Level II recording.

Measured Drawings

Like the Level III recordation, a Level II project may require measured drawings. It is not difficult to measure a structure and sketch it on a artist's pad. The basic dimensions are recorded, along with details such as the size of openings for windows and doors. Notes are made as to windows (how many lights per window), doors, and construction/architectural details.

The field sketches are redrafted into a scale drawing (often 1/4 inch equals 1 foot). This work can be done by most anyone who has some basic drafting skills. It is also possible to generate these drawings using graphics programs on a computer. For instance an Apple MacIntosh computer with Adobe Illustrator software can create scale drawings.

The primary difference between a Level II measured drawing and the more formal HABS/HAER documention is that special HABS mylar is not used, an architect does not necessarily do the measured drawings, and they can be done on either archival paper or mylar. Level II measured drawings can be placed on mylar for archival permanence. These drawings may also be made on archival bond paper (this is especially true using a computer), which will provide long term permanence.

Generally, Level II drawings are much more simple than HABS/HAERs. They are normally for "lesser" structures, and they can be done by most anyone with a pencil and artist's sketch pad. Level II measured drawings are a good way to dimensionally represent a historic property without having to create HABS/HAER architectural plans.

Photographic Documentation

Like Level III recordation, archival photography is important to fully document an historic property. As noted, 35mm film is not particularly good for detailed recording. A larger film format will capture details while allowing for enlargement of negatives without significant quality loss. HABS/HAER requires no less than 4 by 5 inch negatives. In addition to perspective corrections which a view camera can do, the level of detail on a large negative is significantly higher than a small format.

Level II photography is a compromise between small format and large format negatives. Using cameras that require 120 size film, various sizes of negatives can be created. Standard formats are 6 centimeters by 6 centimeters [2 1/4 inches by 2 1/4 inches], 6 centimeters by 7 centimeters, 6 centimeters by 8 centimeters and 6 centimeters by 4.5 centimeters. All of these formats use 120 size film and have attributes that are suitable for mid-level archival photographs.

Level II photography, with a medium format camera, allows for detailed recording of a historic property, without the expense and difficulty of a 4 x 5 (or larger) view camera. Medium format equipment is often more assessable and may be used by photographers who are less proficient than needed to use a large format camera. The only serious limitation to Level II photodocumentation is that medium format cameras cannot normally be shifted to correct for distortion and perspective. There are some cameras that can use special adapters that permit perspective correction. For instance a Zorkendorfer adapter creates limited lens shift. However, such equipment is very expensive and probably not cost-effective for Level II photography.

A typical "medium format" negative is 2 1/4 by 2 1/4 inches.

Level III Documentation

This is the formal process of Historic American Buildings Surveys or Historic American Engineering Records. As described in Chapter II, Level III documentation is extremely precise and requires multiple professional skills. HABS/HAER recordation for a historic property is normally reserved for those sites that are of considerable significance, both historically and architecturally. HABS/HAER is also appropriate for mitigation of major historic sites (i.e. those eligible for the National Register of Historic Places) that also contain architectural importance.

Conclusions

Historic properties should always have a Level I record prepared for them. The basic record that all sites must have are critical because without a file record, the site literally "does not exist". Both present and future researchers will not know about historic properties unless they are recorded for permanent files.

Level II documentation is a good way to create archival records for a historic property when more than a Level I record is needed. This can happen when a site must be mitigated due to impending loss, when a site should be recorded because it is deteriorating and must be "frozen in time" before it further erodes, when a site must be documented, but Level III documentation is not warranted, and anytime a historic property should be documented on an archival basis.

Level III documentation is reserved for the "best" historic properties. These are architecturally important places or are sites that represent significant engineering accomplishments. In some cases, what appear to be "insignificant" properties can be very important historically and should be documented at the HABS/HAER level. The determination as to whether a historic property should have Level III documentation performed is based upon consultation with the State Historic Preservation Officer and the regional HABS/HAER office of the National Park Service. Often, this discussion will result in a Level II record as being satisfactory to mitigate a site. Sometimes, HABS/HAER will suggest photographs and historical documentation, with "field drawings" providing the architectural plans. The field drawings are not formal architectural drawings, but are satisfactory for properties that are not suitable for total HABS/HAER documentation.

PART FOUR

PRESERVING HISTORIC PLACES

ON FILM

Part IV
The Preservation of Historic Sites on Film

There are innumerable historic properties that can be "saved" on film. Many of these sites are typical of a time, type, style, or era and are perfect candidates for archival photographs. Historic places too can be preserved on film. Landscapes, streetscapes, urban settings, battlefields, and other man made modifications to the environmental are worthy of photography to record them in time. To simplify the process of determining what types of historic properties should be recorded, the following guidelines discuss various site types.

This 1890s home in Lake City, Colorado is what should be preserved on film.

<u>Structures/Buildings</u>

Photographing architectural sites is not particularly difficult if it is understood that the main goal is to fully document the property. This means that not only is the primary feature photographed, but also all ancillary properties must be documented. The relationships of structures and features are as important as just the architectural information. Equally, the environmental setting as it relates to the historic properties must be adequately considered.

At the least, the following photos should be made for most architectural historic properties:

1. All fours sides of the primary feature.

2. Three-quarter views of each corner of the principle feature.

3. Detailed views such as windows, doors, unusual features, construction style and so forth of the main feature.

4. Views that show materials used in construction of the primary feature.

5. An overall view of the primary feature showing how it relates to other buildings/environmental settings.

6. At least two three-quarter views of each outbuilding or smaller feature on the property. This will assure that all sides of lesser properties will be documented.

7. Appropriate views that shows how outbuildings and other features relate to each other.

8. Views of unique or special details of outbuildings, foundations, and other features that may not be obvious in over-all photographs.

The more complex a site, more photographs will be needed. Trying to save film by photographing the minimum number of views to document a site is false economy. Film is relatively inexpensive in relationship to time and equipment. It is far more expensive to have to go back to a site and shoot more photos than it is to have more than you need when you leave. The use of a good quality tripod will assure steady exposures that ANY handheld camera simply cannot give. It is very strongly recommended that a tripod be used for all exposures. It makes good sense to shoot at least two exposures of each view. This provides "insurance" that at least one exposure will be printable. Based on a meter reading, one main shot can be made. Then exposures on either side of that reading should be made and the photos taken. That will give the photographer a "bracket" of exposures; one f/stop "overexposed" and one f/stop "underexposed". For example if the light meter calls for f/11 at 125th of a second, a bracket would be f/8 at 125th and f/16 at 125th.

The use of filters is very advisable when photographing architectural sites. Filters enhance details and bring out surfaces that might otherwise go unnoticed. One of the most useful filters is a Medium Yellow (Y2) that increases contrast and helps define surfaces such as wood, brick, and logs. Other filters like orange enhance the yellow filter effect even more. Green filters tend to enhance foliage and plants, while a red filter will provide a "night" effect. Photos shot with a red filter look like they were taken at night under a full moon.

Another useful filter is the polarizer. When glare, or reflection is a problem a polarizing filter is used to reduce or eliminate refraction. This is particularly helpful if the photograph involves bodies of water, or large areas of glass. Using a polarizer makes it possible to shoot through glass or into a situation where there is considerable glare. The same applies to scenes involving snow glare.

While color films are not suitable for archival quality photographs, there are times that the medium must be used. Filters can also enhance color photos. A polarizer not only reduces glare and refraction, but also tends to enrich colors. For example, polarizers make a blue sky much darker and more intense. Other useful filters include a "warming filter" like an 81A which creates warmer colors. This is helpful in shadows and other situations where the scene is too "cold".

A simple and effective way by which to increase photographic quality is to use a lens shade (hood) for all shots. A lens hood reduces flare and distortion, resulting in sharper, crisper photographs. A lens hood should be mandatory for ALL lenses.

Engineering Features

Historic engineering properties can include everything from dams to mining stamp mills and industrial processes (i.e. steelmaking). Photographing such sites can be difficult because the goal is to impart not only what the features look like, but also what their purpose is/was. There are no set rules for photographing industrial or engineering properties because each one is different and has certain idiosyncracies. There are probably no two engineering or industrial sites that are exactly alike.

Generally, there are several basic features that should be recorded. They include:

1. An over-all view of the site that shows the relationship between various components.

2. The significant features of the site that are discussed in the historical documentation of the property.

35

3. The architectural aspects of the property should be photographed. This is similar to the documentation of buildings (above), and involves the same types of views.

4. The technical aspects of the property should be documented. For instance, in a stamp mill, the various components such as the stamps, ovens, tables, vats, etc. should be photographed.

5. Both interior and exterior photographs should show details of design of construction, including structural systems, and special features of the building/site.

6. Smaller "detail" shots should be made that show machinery, tools, specific processes, and other intricate parts of the building's technology.

Industrial sites are unique subjects as this photo of the Hanson Mill in San Juan County, Colorado shows.

7. The structure's exterior and interior should be covered from as many angles as possible. In this way, one part of a machine or process may be related to other equipment in the room.

8. If historical photos of the property are available, they should be archivally copied and included in the photo documentation process. This is particularly true of industrial/engineering sites where the property may have been photographed when new, but has been substantially changed, or destroyed, over the years.

An historic photo taken near Aspen, Colorado shows how the site looked in the 1890s. (J. E. Spurr Photo U.S. Geological Survey)

The same "rules" apply to photographing engineering/industrial features as architectural sites. Filters should be used to enhance details, polarizers for refraction control, and a tripod should always be available to provide for rock steady exposures.

Bridges and Trestles

Unlike industrial/engineering features, bridges and trestles do not normally have features for production of goods. Rather, they are transportation systems for moving goods and people. Bridges and trestles can be for railways, roads, and automobiles. Photographing bridges requires that certain basic views are covered. They should include:

1. An overall view of the span(s) should be taken. This can present something of a challenge if the bridge is very long. A wide-angle lens is most valuable in giving adequate coverage for really long bridges.

2. Views of the structural systems of a bridge/trestle should be photographed. Truss types, connections between components, pilings, and abutments and other features should be recorded.

3. Detailed shots of specific features such as builder's plates, rivets, bolts, flanges, and other materials should be made.

4. Materials used in various parts of the structure (such as decking) should be photographed.

The Whiskey Creek Trestle (Uintah Railway) is an example of an ordinary narrow gauge bridge.

38

As in the case of engineering and architectural properties, the use of filters, tripods, and other equipment will assure quality archival photographs. Bridges and trestles are unique and challenging features that deserve careful recordation because older sites are disappearing at a rapid rate, only to be replaced by low-spans of little architectural merit.

Railroads

Railways are unique engineering and architectural features that must be recorded in ways that do not apply to other types of sites. First, a railroad is a linear feature with subcomponents of engineering features along the right-of-way. Secondly, there are numerous structures associated with a railroad such as stations, roundhouses, yards, water towers, section houses, freight houses, bridges, and other architectural features. Thirdly, a railroad uses rolling stock to move goods and people. This includes passenger cars, freight cars, locomotives, and specialized equipment like snow plows and flangers. Thus, recording a railroad, or parts of a railway, can be complex. Depending upon the scope of a project, the following features should generally be documented:

> 1. Linear features such as a railroad line (either operational or abandoned) should include a view down the roadbed, making sure that converging lines do not occur. A view camera will permit this kind of photograph. Additionally, any engineering features such as cuts, fills, tunnels, or crossings of drainages should be documented. Not every drainage is crossed by a bridge or trestle. Some very interesting stone culverts are often used by railroads.

This Rio Grande Southern narrow gauge railbed at Lizard Head Pass is still visible.

39

2. Architectural features such as stations, outbuildings, water towers, freight houses, section houses, signal towers, guard houses, sheds, locomotive sheds, roundhouses, turntables, and other buildings or structures should be recorded using the same guidelines as for architectural properties. Views showing relationships between buildings are important, as are shots of the structures, and other features. If a rail yard is involved, the interrelationships between the architectural features and the layout of the yard should be documented.

3. Bridges and trestles are recorded as described in the section on bridges (above).

4. Other features like tunnels can be recorded using flash equipment to light the interior. The primary information within a tunnel is the construction detail, for example wooden timbers used to shore up the structure. Sometimes it is also possible to record the "historic soot" on the roof of the tunnel. The portals of a tunnel should also be photographed as should the approaches. Sometimes the portals are nothing but the rock into which the tunnel was blasted. In other cases, they can be elaborate edifices.

Railroad outbuildings like this water tower and station at Sargents, Colorado are links to railroading's past.

Generally, railroads are one of the most complex historic features to record. Often they are still in use, despite being very historic in quality. Recordation of "operating" railroads calls for great caution because trains cannot always be heard. Not to mention it is trespassing to get on the right-of-way along an existing railway. The same guidelines for exposures apply to railroads. Filters, tripods, and other equipment will help make for top-quality archival photos.

Roads and Trails

Similar to railroads, trails and roads are linear features that may or may not have architectural sites connected with them. Equally, they may have engineering qualities that make them special. Like railways, certain shots should be taken to assure coverage of the site:

> 1. A view of the length (or portion of the length) of the road/trail should be made. Like a railroad, converging lines should be eliminated with the use of a view camera. Details of special features should also be photographed. For example, if the road is made of a unique asphalt, it should be recorded.

> 2. View of cuts, fills, culverts, bridges, trestles, and other engineering features should be made. These are similar to railway features and can be treated in the same way.

> 3. Detailed views of roads/trails should be made to document special or unique parts of the site. Such shots might include ruts, wagon tire marks (in rock most likely), pavements (asphalt, brick, macadam, etc.), and other small features.

> 4. If there are associated structures along and road/trail, they too should be recorded. If the sites are architectural in quality, they should be photographed using the guidelines for buildings (above). If the features are in ruins, they should be photographed according to the suggestions for historical archaeological sites.

As in the case of other historic properties, the use of filters, tripods, and other equipment assures quality photographs.

Landscapes/Streetscapes

Landscapes (and streetscapes) are unusual in that very often they involve recording all of the above features. A streetscape is urban in concept and involves recording buildings, roads, and other man-made features in a city or town setting. A landscape is usually a photograph of nature, be it man-manipulated or natural. The same guidelines apply to either type of photograph since they are intended to record a wider scene than specific features:

1. A wide-angle lens is good for landscapes/streetscapes because it provides a considerable angle of view thus taking in the over-all scene. The environmental setting is hence recorded, as are man-made changes to the area. A landscape is supposed to be an overview, not a specific shot.

2. There may also be details to be recorded. In the case of a planned landscape (such as a city park), various architectural features should be recorded, including benches, statues, flower beds, paths, trails, gazebos, etc.

A streetscape of Victor, Colorado in 1974 gives an indication of the past.

As with the photography of other historical features, the proper use of lenses, filters, tripods, and other equipment assures good quality photographs.

Historical Archaeology

Historical archaeological sites are different than historic sites because they are usually not standing but rather are subsurface features. These kinds of sites include can dumps, trash pits, outhouse pits, cellars, foundations, and other subsurface manifestations. Photographing these kinds of sites involves close-ups, photos made in pits and excavation, requiring flash equipment, and sometimes aerial photos are needed to show large areas of a site complex. In general, photographing archaeological sites is a different proposition than standing structures. The requirements for archival permanence may be the same, but the photo techniques are not.

At a minimum the following shots should be made for a historical archaeological site:

1. Over-all view of the site and the relationship between and among components.

2. Views of excavations that will reveal the extent of the work being undertaken.

3. Detailed views of stratification, artifacts, etc. that are photographed within context and that show how the materials lie in the soil.

4. Views of the environmental setting for the site/features. This can include vegetation, soils, geography, and other important features.

To a large extent, archaeology depends on color reproduction for research. Black and white photos do not always tell soil colors, stains, vegetation types, and other vital scientific information. Therefore, many archaeologists prefer color films. The use of color precludes archival quality photographs. If color must be used, it should be done with "archivally stable" films like Kodachrome and printed on Cibachrome papers. If properly stored, the transparencies should last at least 100 years. Other color films (positive or negative) will probably not last more than 30 years.

Other Historic Features and Ruins

In many cases, none of the above categories will apply to an historic site. It may be in ruins, or it just may be a foundation with a few depression around the main feature. In these cases, an application of archaeology photography and architectural recording is appropriate. The same principles apply to photographing ruins or minimal features. There should be at least the following photographs made to assure that the feature is thoroughly recorded:

1. View of over-all site, including main feature(s) and outlying features.

2. Views of each primary feature such as a foundation, outbuilding, collapsed structure, or other semi-standing features.

3. Three quarter views of foundations, cellars, etc. This assures that all angles of the site are covered.

4. Detailed close-ups of special or unique site features such as can dumps, outhouse remains, special equipment or artifacts, etc.

5. Views of the environmental setting showing relationships between physical features and the environment in which they sit.

Even ruins like the Crest House on Mount Evans, Colorado can tell a story.

Conclusions

There are many kinds of historic properties that may be recorded for the future. While this list is in no way complete, the ideas expressed will apply to a vast majority of historic sites. By using the guidelines for each type of site, along with proper processing and photographic techniques, anyone should be able to minimally record historic properties. While the quality may not be HABS/HAER, the photographs, if archivally finished, will last hundreds of years. The site can live on into the future on film and paper, if not in reality.

The contribution of photographers to historic preservation is considerable. Without photographs, we would have a much harder time visualizing the past. Future generations can have the advantage of knowing what our times looked like because someone correctly photographed both current and older places. Recording historic properties builds a legacy of preservation that is a major addition to the body of knowledge. With a little practice and experience, most any photographer can help increase our awareness of both the past and the present. We hope that this book will give photographers and those interested in historic preservation a few ideas on preserving both the present and the past on film.

Small structures like the Horseshoe Ranger Station make good subjects for recordation.

Sometimes not much is left to record as seen at the San Juan Chief mill near Mineral Point, Colorado.

BIBLIOGRAPHIC REFERENCES

BIBLIOGRAPHY

Athearn, Frederic J. *Habitat In the Past: Historical Perspectives of Riparian Zones on the White River*. (Denver: Bureau of Land Management, 1988.

_____. "Preservation Photography". *Studio Photography*. Volume 17, Number 5, (May, 1981).

Barger, Susan. *Bibliography of Photographic Processes in Use Before 1880: Their Materials, Processing and Conservation*. (Rochester, New York: Rochester Institute of Technology, 1980).

Boucher, Jack E. *A Record in Detail: The Architectural Photographs of Jack E. Boucher*. (Columbia, Missouri: University of Missouri Press, 1988.)

Buchanan, Terry. *Photographing Historic Buildings for the Record*. (London: HMSO, 1983).

Burns, John A. (Ed.) *Recording Historic Structures*. (Washington: American Institute of Architects, 1989).

Casper, Dale E. *Photography and Architecture: Journal Articles, 1982-1988*. (Monticello, Illinois: Vance Bibliographies, 1989).

Clark, Walter. "Caring of Photographs". In: *The Life Library of Photography*. (New York: Time-Life Books, 1972). Volume 17.

Coe, Brian. *The Birth of Photography--The Story of the Formative Years, 1800-1900*. (London: Ash and Grant, 1976).

Dean, Jeff. *Architectural Photography: Techniques for Architects, Preservationists, Historians, Photographers, and Urban Planners*. (Nashville: American Association for State and Local History, 1981).

De Mare, Eric S. *Photography and Architecture*. (New York: Praeger, 1961).

Dorrell, Peter G. *Photography in Archaeology and Conservation*. (Cambridge: Cambridge University Press, 1989).

Doumato, Lamia. *Architecture and Photography*. (Monticello, Illinois: Vance Bibliographies, 1987).

Eastman Kodak Company. *Conservation of Photographs*. (Rochester, New York: Kodak, 1985).

_____. *Photography With Large-Format Cameras*. (Rochester, New York: Kodak, 1973).

Jeffrey, Ian. "Photography: Representing the Present". *Annals of the Architectural Association*. (Fall, 1988, p. 52).

Mangan, Terry W. *Caring For Photographs: Archival Collecting of Photography For Small Museums*. (Denver: State Historical Society of Colorado, 1975).

McGrath, Norman. *Photographing Buildings Inside and Out*. (New York: Whitney Libary of Design, 1987).

McKee, Harley J. *Recording Historic Buildings*. (Washington, D.C.: Government Printing Office, 1970).

Miner, Ralph W. *Conservation of Historical and Cultural Resources*. (Chicago: American Society of Planning Officials, 1969).

Molitor, Joseph W. *Architectural Photography*. (New York: Wiley, 1976).

Morgan, William. *Portals: Photographs*. Dublin, N.H.: William L. Bauhan, 1981).

National Park Serivce. *Transmitting Documentation to HABS/HAER/WASO*. (Washington, D.C.: National Park Service, 1985).

_____. *Field Instructions for Measured Drawings*. (Washington, D.C.: Natonal Park Service, n.d.)

_____. *Specifications for the Production of Photographs*. (Washington, D.C.: National Park Service, n.d.).

_____. *Manual for Editing HABS/HAER Documentation*. (Denver: Rocky Mountain Regional Office, 1986).

Oliver, Joe. "Architectural Photocomposition". *Photomethods*. Volume 32, p. 34 (March, 1989).

Orth, Thomas. *A Selected Bibliography on Photographic Conservation*. (Rochester, New York: Rochester Institute of Technology, 1981).

Ostroff, Eugene. *Conserving and Restoring Photographic Collections*. Washington: American Association of Museums, 1975.

_____. "Preservation of Photographs". *Photographic Journal* (Royal Photographic Society). Volume 107 (October, 1967), pp.309-314.

_____. "Photographic Preservation: Modern Techniques". *Royal Photographic Symposium*, 1974.

Plowden, David. *Bridges: The Spans of North America*. (New York: Viking Press, 1974.)

_____. *Industrial Landscape*. (Chicago: Chicago Historical Association, 1985.)

Robinson, Cervin. *Architecture Transformed: A History of the Photography of Buildings from 1839 to the Present*. (New York: Architectural League of New York, MIT Press, 1987).

Shulman, Julius. *The Photography of Architecture and Design: Photographing Buildings, Interiors, and the Visual Arts*. (New York: Whitney Library of Design, 1977.)

Vance, Mary A. *Architectural Photography: A Bibliography*. (Monticello, Illinois: Vance Bibliographies, 1981).

Weinstein, Robert A. and Larry Booth. *The Collection, Use and Care of Historical Photographs*. (Nashville: American Association of State and Local History, 1977).

White, Anthony G. *Architectural Photography: A Selected Bibliography*. (Monticello,Illinois: Vance Bibliographies, 1983).

FOLIOS OF HABS AND HAERS

FOLIO ONE

THE ASPEN LUMBER COMPANY

HISTORIC AMERICAN BUILDINGS SURVEY

DRAWINGS AND PHOTOGRAPHS

THE ASPEN LUMBER COMPANY BUILDING

THIS BUILDING DATED FROM ABOUT 1895 AND REPRESENTED ONE OF THE OLDEST WOODEN STRUCTURES IN ASPEN, COLORADO. THE PROPERTY WAS FIRST OWNED BY W. C. E. KOCH WHO IS SHOWN AS OWNER OF RECORD IN 1880. THE BUILDING FIRST APPEARS ON TOWN MAPS IN 1896 (WILLIT'S MAP). THE BLOCK UPON WHICH THE ASPEN LUMBER COMPANY SITS WAS PASSED THROUGH THE KOCH FAMILY TO 1968 WHEN DOROTHY KOCH SHAW IS SHOWN AS THE OWNER. IN 1979 HANS CANTRUP PURCHASED THE KOCH LUMBER BLOCK. THE KOCH LUMBER COMPANY BUILDINGS WERE DEMOLISHED IN SEPTEMBER, 1980. THE ASPEN LUMBER COMPANY BUILDING WAS PARTLY IN TRESPASS ON BUREAU OF LAND MANAGEMENT LAND, BECAUSE THE FACADE WAS ON FEDERAL LAND, THE CITY OF ASPEN STOPPED THE DEMOLITION OF THIS SITE. UPON AGREEMENT BETWEEN HANS CANTRUP, THE CITY OF ASPEN, BLM, AND THE ASPEN HISTORICAL SOCIETY; THE SITE WAS RECORDED.

THIS BUILDING WAS FIRST USED AS A STABLE AND/OR LIVERY BARN. LATER IT SEEMS TO HAVE BEEN A STORAGE BARN FOR THE KOCH LUMBER COMPANY. A SHED WAS ADDED TO THE WEST SIDE OF THE STRUCTURE ABOUT 1896. THE ASPEN LUMBER COMPANY BUILDINGS' PRIMARY FEATURES ARE ITS CLAPBOARD FACADE WITH "OLD STYLE" LETTERING, AND ITS MIXTURE OF BUILDING MATERIALS. THE FACADE IS CLAPBOARD, WHILE THE SIDES AND REAR ARE BOARD AND BATTEN CONSTRUCTION. THE ROOF WAS ORIGINALLY CEDAR SHINGLE, BUT WAS RE-ROOFED WITH GALVINIZED CORRUGATED STEEL AT A LATER DATE. THE ADDITIONAL SHED WAS ALSO BOARD AND BATTEN CONSTRUCTION WITH A METAL ROOF. THESE STRUCTURES WERE BOTH IN BADLY DETERIORATED CONDITION IN 1980, HAVING BEEN ABANDONED FOR MANY YEARS. THE ASPEN LUMBER COMPANY BUILDINGS WERE DEMOLISHED IN OCTOBER, 1980.

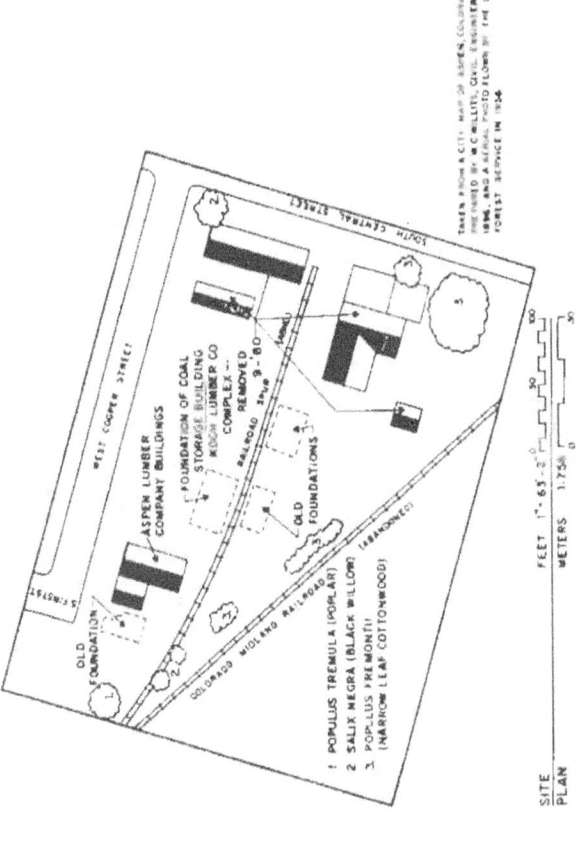

SITE PLAN

FEET 1"= 63'-2"
METERS 1:750

1. POPULUS TREMULA (POPLAR)
2. SALIX NEGRA (BLACK WILLOW)
3. POP.LUS FREMONT(I) (NARROW LEAF COTTONWOOD)

LOCATION MAP

THE FIELDWORK, PHOTOGRAPHS, HISTORICAL DATA, AND MEASURED DRAWINGS WERE PREPARED UNDER THE DIRECTION OF FREDERIC J. ATHEARN, STATE HISTORIAN OF THE BUREAU OF LAND MANAGEMENT, COLORADO (UNIVERSITY OF TEXAS, AUSTIN). MEASURED DRAWINGS WERE PREPARED BY LEIGH A. WELLBORN, ARCHITECT, BUREAU OF LAND MANAGEMENT, COLORADO (UNIVERSITY OF KANSAS). PHOTOGRAPHS WERE TAKEN BY FREDERIC J. ATHEARN. FINAL DELINATION OF THE MEASURED DRAWINGS WAS DONE BY STEVEN W. GREBE, DELINEATOR, BUREAU OF LAND MANAGEMENT, COLORADO (STATE UNIVERSITY OF NEW YORK, BINGHAMTON).

DRAWN BY LEIGH A. WELLBORN, ARCHITECT and STEVEN W GREBE, DEL., 1982

C.S.D. BUREAU OF LAND MANAGEMENT
OFFICE OF ARCHEOLOGY AND HISTORIC PRESERVATION
NATIONAL PARK SERVICE
UNITED STATES DEPARTMENT OF THE INTERIOR

ASPEN LUMBER COMPANY
CORNER OF WEST COOPER AND SOUTH FIRST STREETS, ASPEN, PITKIN COUNTY, COLORADO

SURVEY NO	
CO-61	HISTORIC AMERICAN BUILDINGS SURVEY
	SHEET 1 OF 5 SHEETS

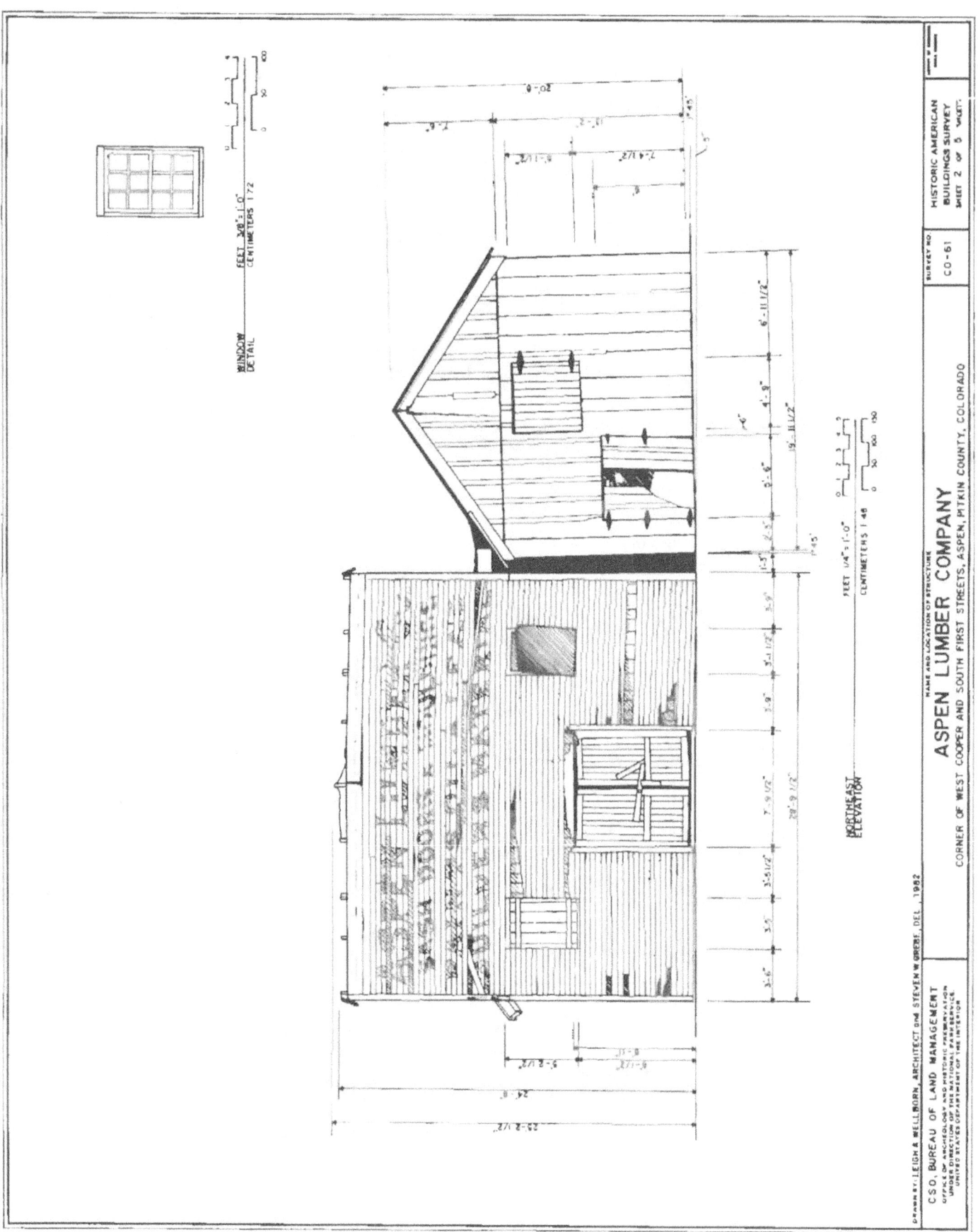

WINDOW
DETAIL

FEET 3/8"=1'-0"

CENTIMETERS 1:72

NORTHEAST
ELEVATION

FEET 1/4"=1'-0"

CENTIMETERS 1:48

DRAWN BY: LEIGH A. WELLBORN, ARCHITECT and STEVEN W. GREBE, DEL. 1982

CSO, BUREAU OF LAND MANAGEMENT

OFFICE OF ARCHEOLOGY AND HISTORIC PRESERVATION
UNDER DIRECTION OF THE NATIONAL PARK SERVICE
UNITED STATES DEPARTMENT OF THE INTERIOR

NAME AND LOCATION OF STRUCTURE

ASPEN LUMBER COMPANY

CORNER OF WEST COOPER AND SOUTH FIRST STREETS, ASPEN, PITKIN COUNTY, COLORADO

SURVEY NO.

CO-61

HISTORIC AMERICAN
BUILDINGS SURVEY

SHEET 2 OF 5 SHEET.

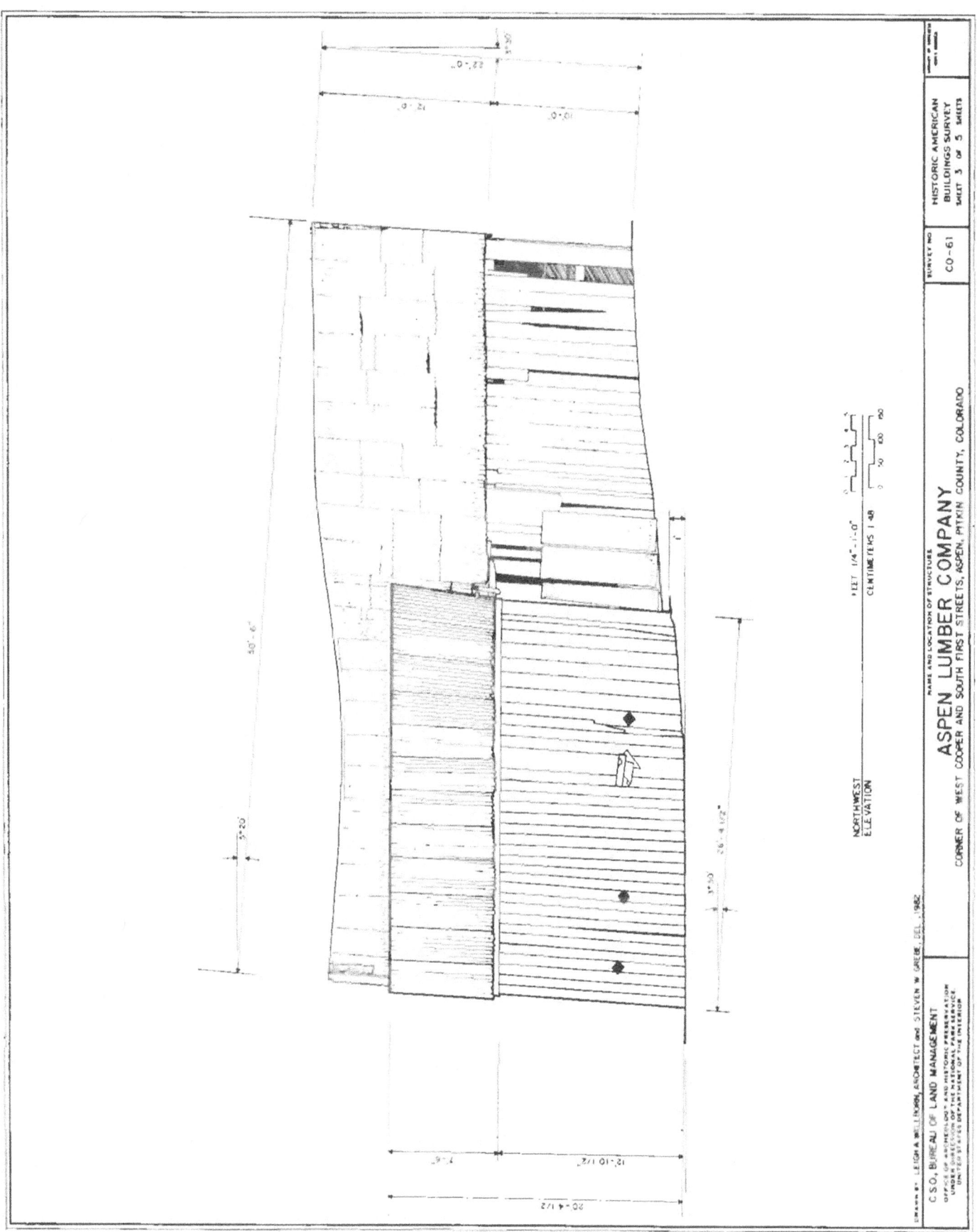

NORTHWEST
ELEVATION

FEET 1/4" = 1'-0"

CENTIMETERS 1:48

ASPEN LUMBER COMPANY

CORNER OF WEST COOPER AND SOUTH FIRST STREETS, ASPEN, PITKIN COUNTY, COLORADO

NAME AND LOCATION OF STRUCTURE

SURVEY NO
CO-61

HISTORIC AMERICAN
BUILDINGS SURVEY
SHEET 3 OF 5 SHEETS

DRAWN BY: LEIGH A. WELLBORN, ARCHITECT and STEVEN W. GREBE, DEL., 1982

C.S.O., BUREAU OF LAND MANAGEMENT

OFFICE OF ARCHEOLOGY AND HISTORIC PRESERVATION
UNDER DIRECTION OF THE NATIONAL PARK SERVICE
UNITED STATES DEPARTMENT OF THE INTERIOR

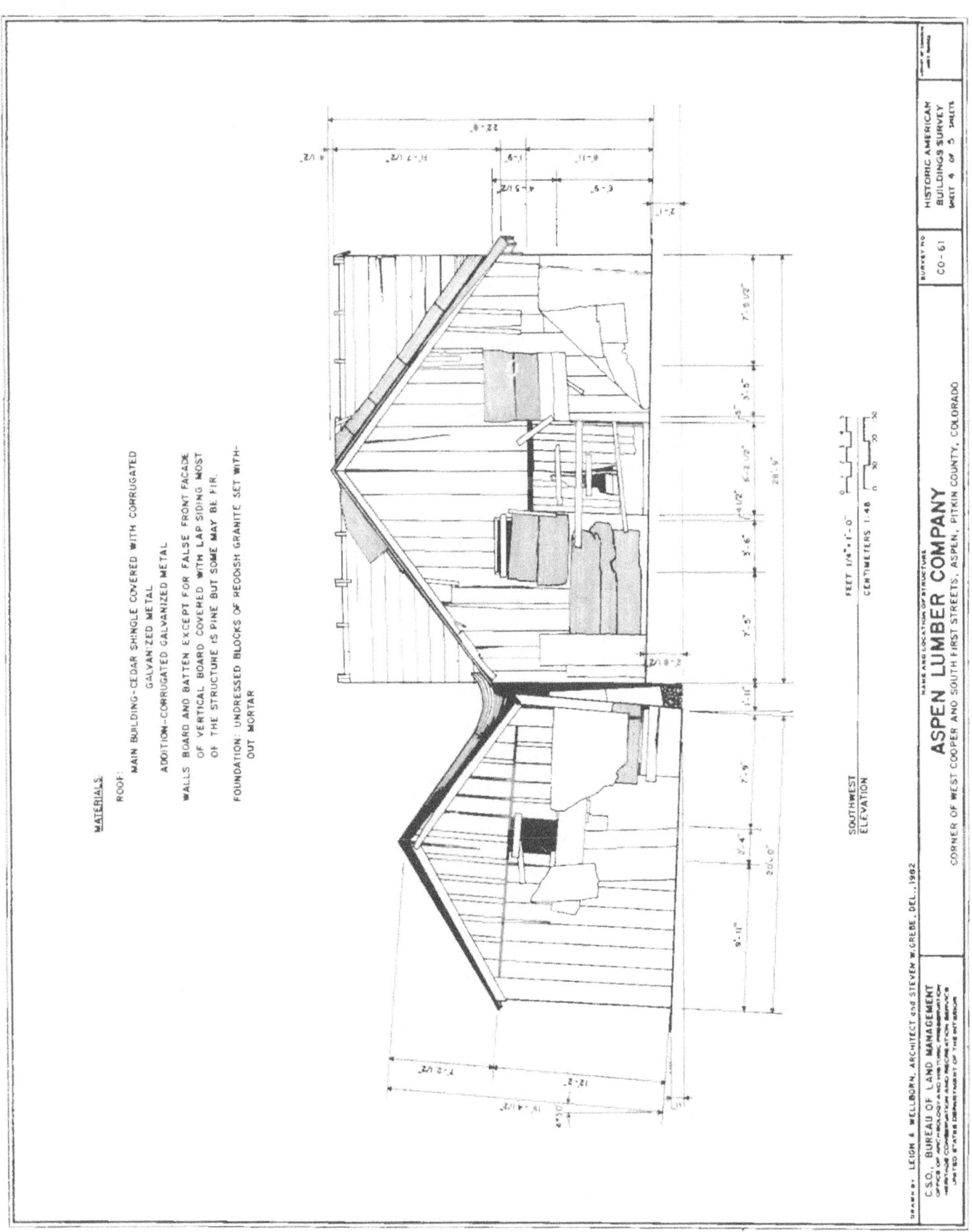

MATERIALS:

ROOF:

MAIN BUILDING-CEDAR SHINGLE COVERED WITH CORRUGATED
GALVANIZED METAL.

ADDITION-CORRUGATED GALVANIZED METAL.

WALLS BOARD AND BATTEN EXCEPT FOR FALSE FRONT FACADE
OF VERTICAL BOARD COVERED WITH LAP SIDING MOST
OF THE STRUCTURE IS PINE BUT SOME MAY BE FIR.

FOUNDATION: UNDRESSED BLOCKS OF REDDISH GRANITE SET WITH-
OUT MORTAR.

SOUTHWEST
ELEVATION

FEET 1/4" = 1'-0"

CENTIMETERS 1:48

DRAWN BY: LEIGH & WELLBORN, ARCHITECT and STEVEN W.GREBE, DEL., 1982

C.S.O., BUREAU OF LAND MANAGEMENT
OFFICE OF ARCHAEOLOGY AND HISTORIC PRESERVATION
HERITAGE CONSERVATION AND RECREATION SERVICE
UNITED STATES DEPARTMENT OF THE INTERIOR

NAME AND LOCATION OF STRUCTURE
ASPEN LUMBER COMPANY
CORNER OF WEST COOPER AND SOUTH FIRST STREETS, ASPEN, PITKIN COUNTY, COLORADO

SURVEY NO.
CO-61

HISTORIC AMERICAN
BUILDINGS SURVEY
SHEET 4 OF 5 SHEETS

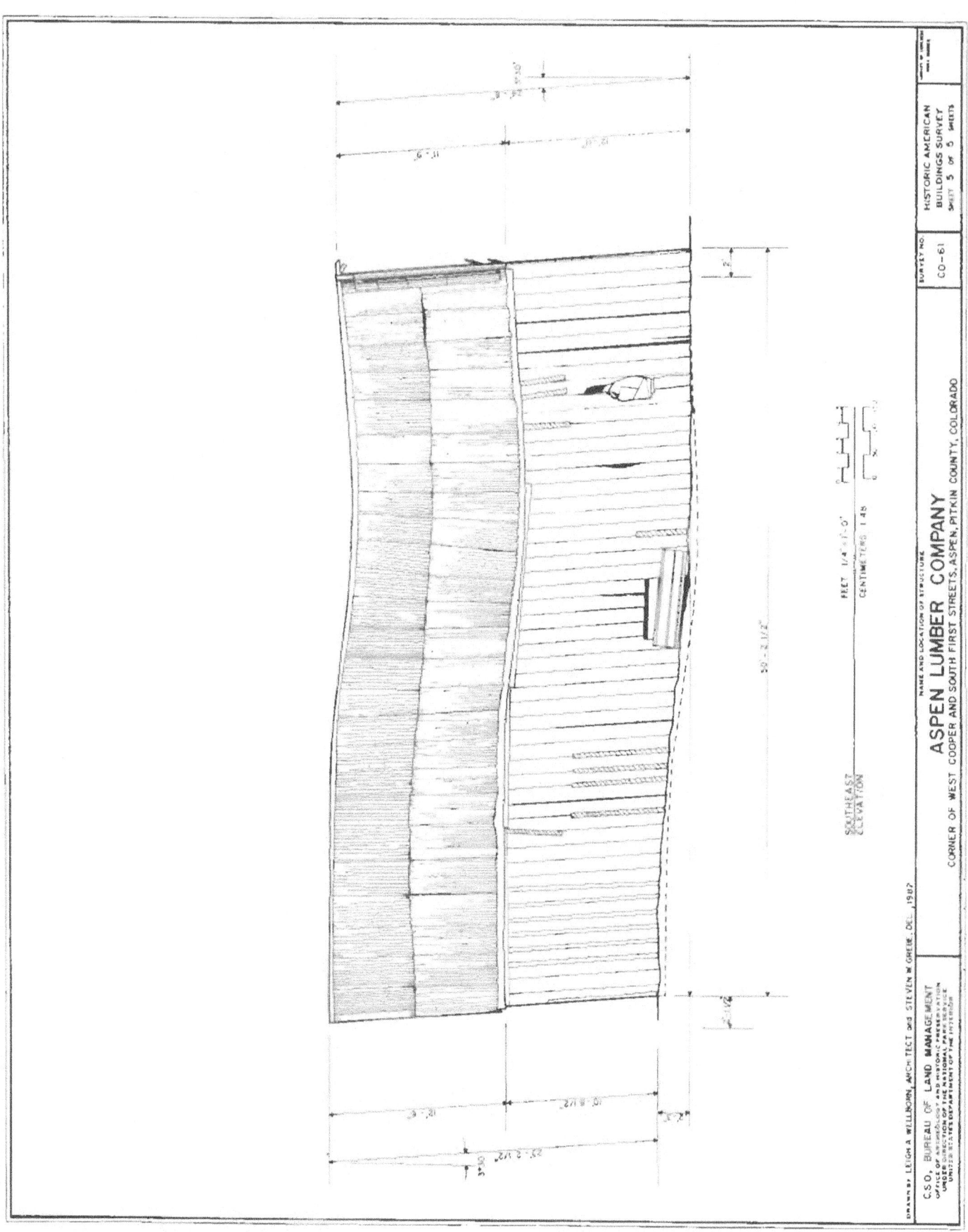

SOUTHEAST
ELEVATION

ASPEN LUMBER COMPANY

CORNER OF WEST COOPER AND SOUTH FIRST STREETS, ASPEN, PITKIN COUNTY, COLORADO

NAME AND LOCATION OF STRUCTURE

C.S.O., BUREAU OF LAND MANAGEMENT
OFFICE OF ARCHEOLOGY AND HISTORIC PRESERVATION
UNDER DIRECTION OF THE NATIONAL PARK SERVICE
UNITED STATES DEPARTMENT OF THE INTERIOR

DRAWN BY: LEIGH A. WELLBORN, ARCHITECT and STEVEN W. GREBE, DEL., 1987

SURVEY NO.
CO-61

HISTORIC AMERICAN
BUILDINGS SURVEY
SHEET 5 OF 5 SHEETS

67

Front of Aspen Lumber Company Building, Facing North

Aspen Lumber Company Building, Facing East

Rear of Aspen Lumber Company Building, Facing South

Aspen Lumber Company Building, Facing West

FOLIO TWO

THE HAVEMEYER-WILLCOX CANAL

HISTORIC AMERICAN ENGINEERING RECORD

DRAWINGS AND PHOTOGRAPHS

HAVEMEYER–WILLCOX
CANAL SYSTEM c.1890–1912

COLORADO

SHARRARD PARK AREA

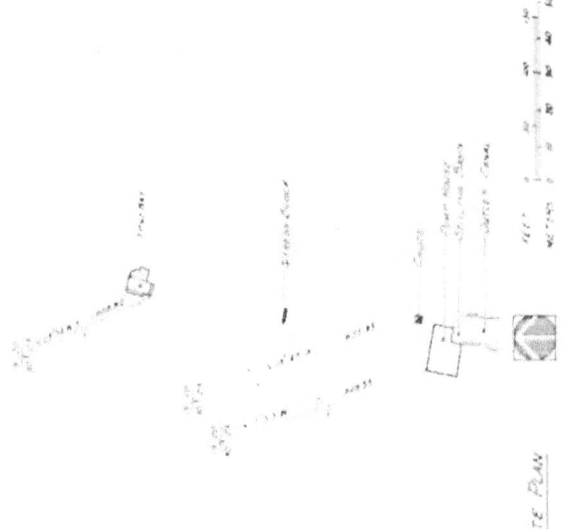

SITE PLAN

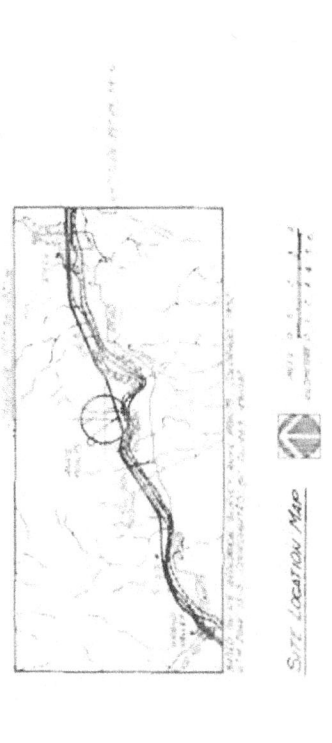

SITE LOCATION MAP

HAVEMEYER-WILLCOX CANAL SYSTEM 1890-1912
GARFIELD COUNTY
COLORADO
SHARRARD PARK AREA

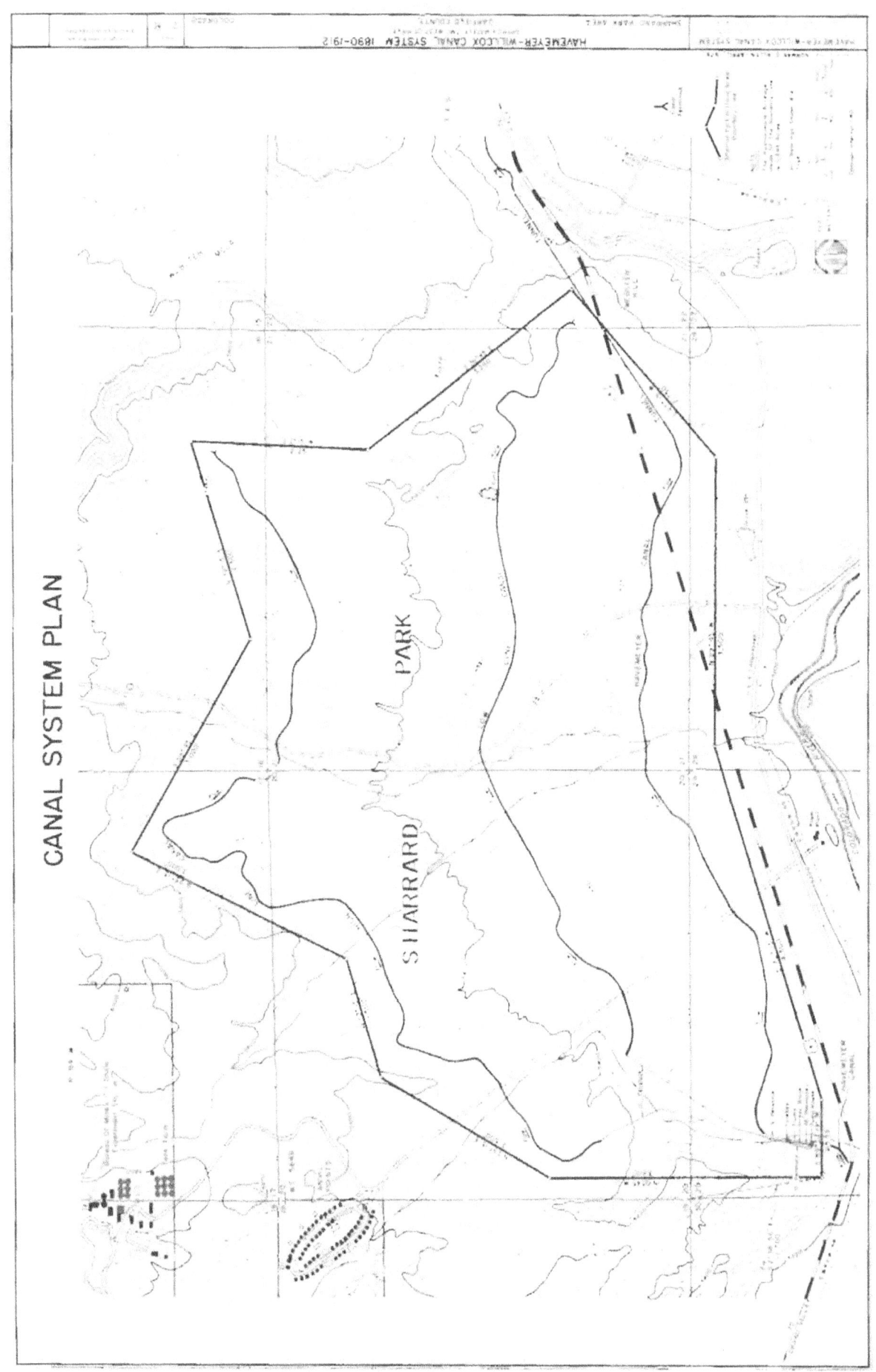

CANAL SYSTEM PLAN

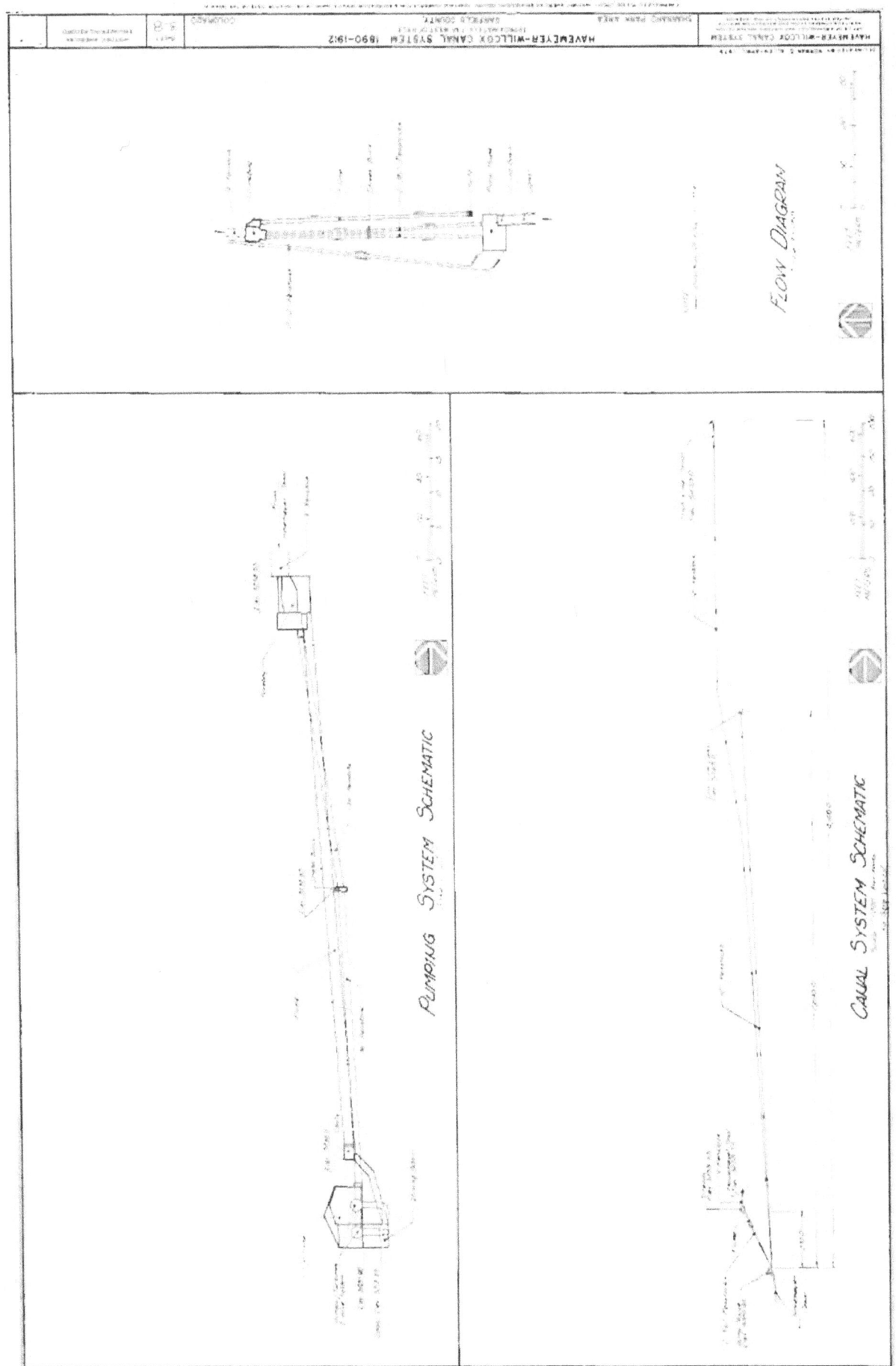

FLOW DIAGRAM

PUMPING SYSTEM SCHEMATIC

CANAL SYSTEM SCHEMATIC

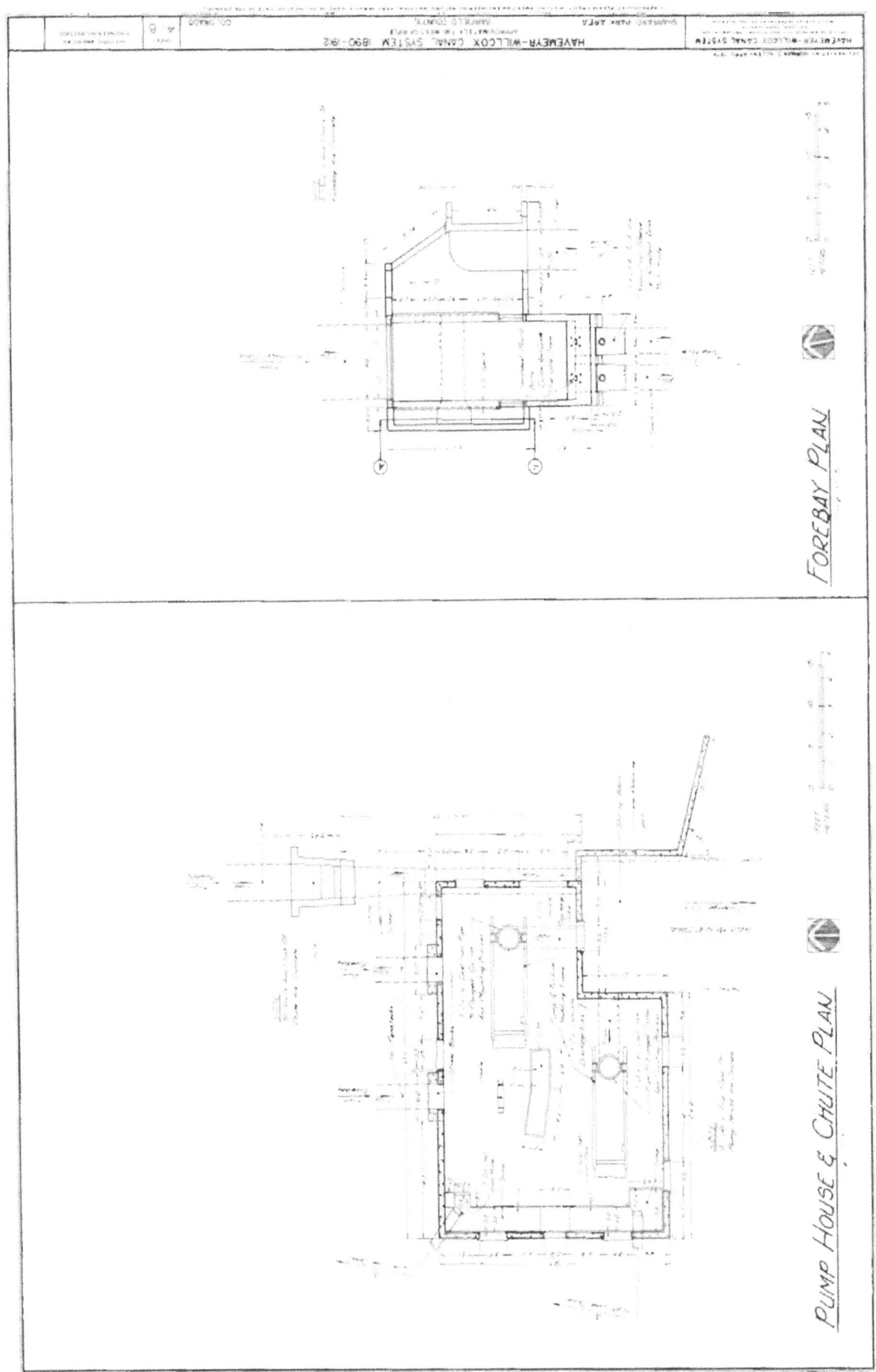

FOREBAY PLAN

PUMP HOUSE & CHUTE PLAN

HAVEMEYER-WILLCOX CANAL SYSTEM 1890-1912

85

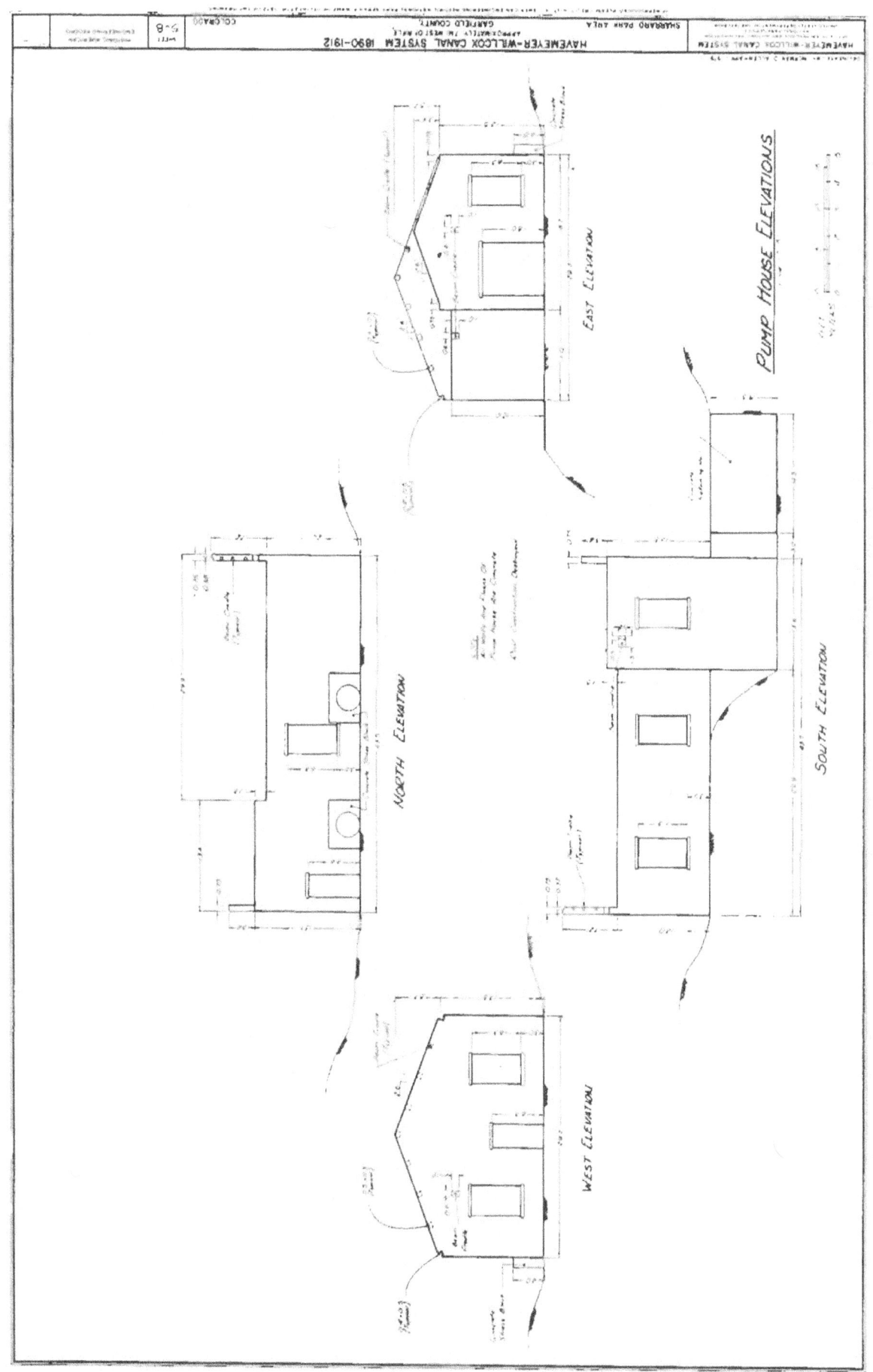

PUMP HOUSE ELEVATIONS

EAST ELEVATION

NORTH ELEVATION

SOUTH ELEVATION

WEST ELEVATION

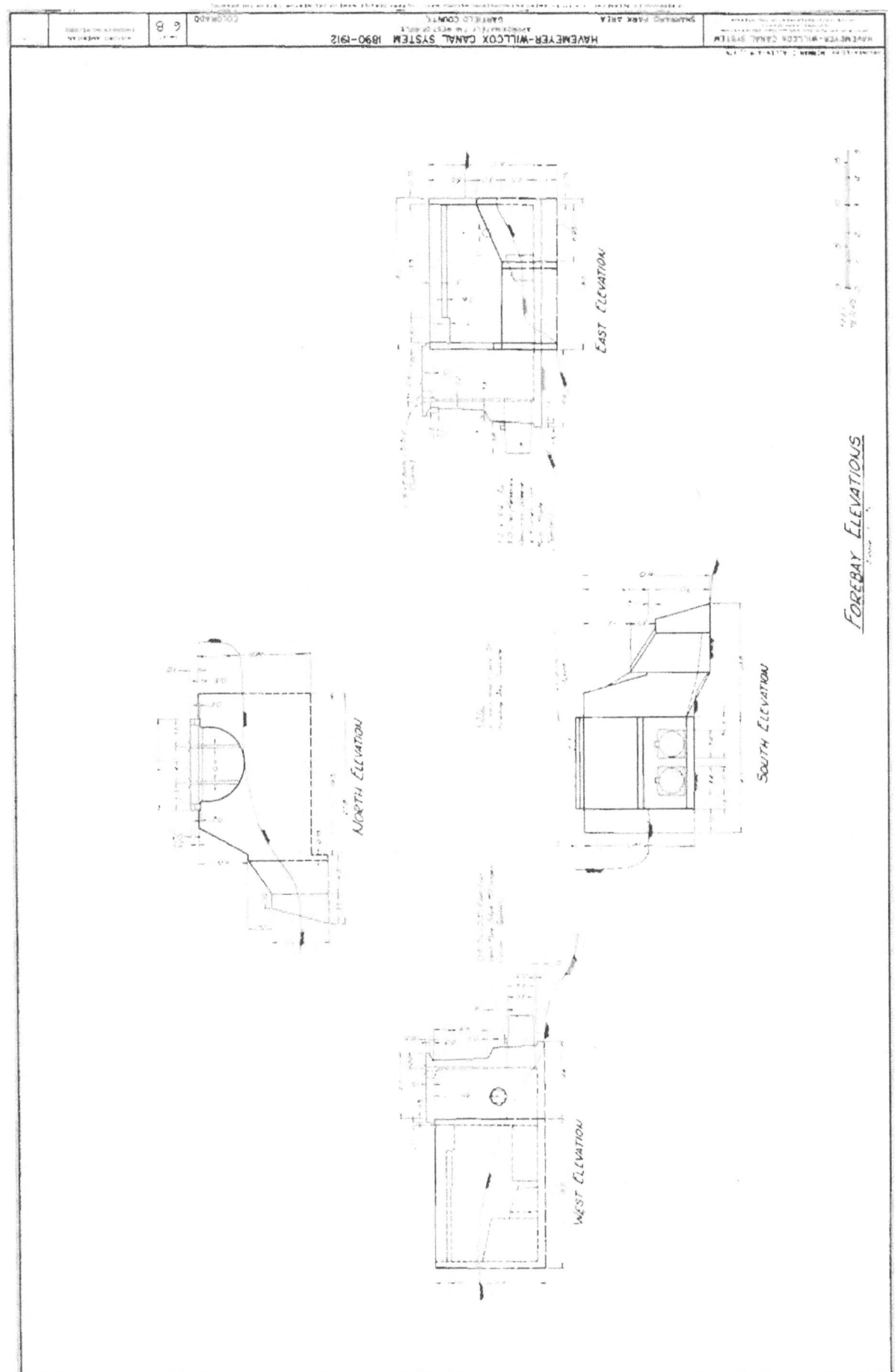

FOREBAY ELEVATIONS

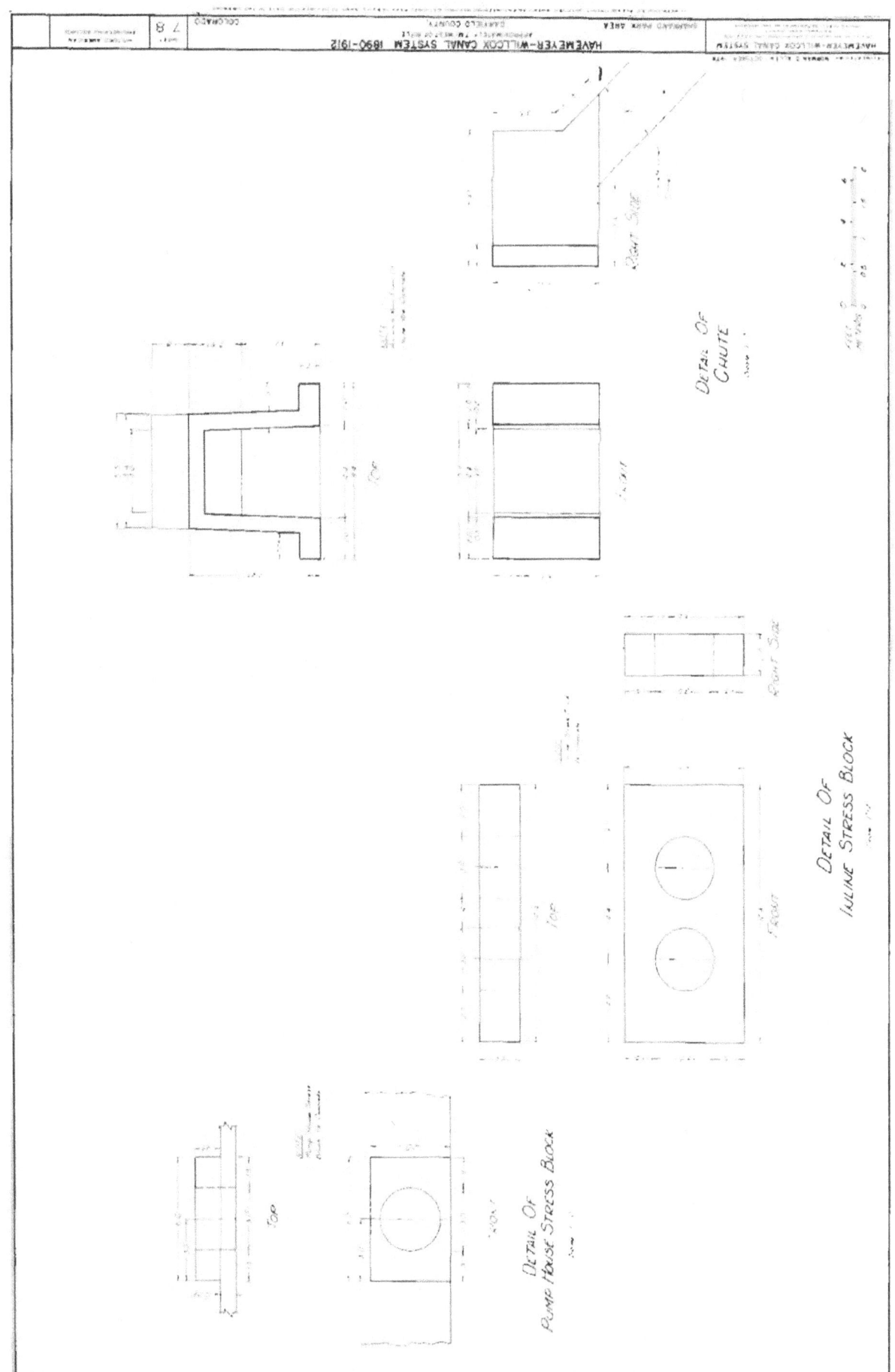

DETAIL OF
CHUTE

DETAIL OF
INLINE STRESS BLOCK

DETAIL OF
PUMP HOUSE STRESS BLOCK

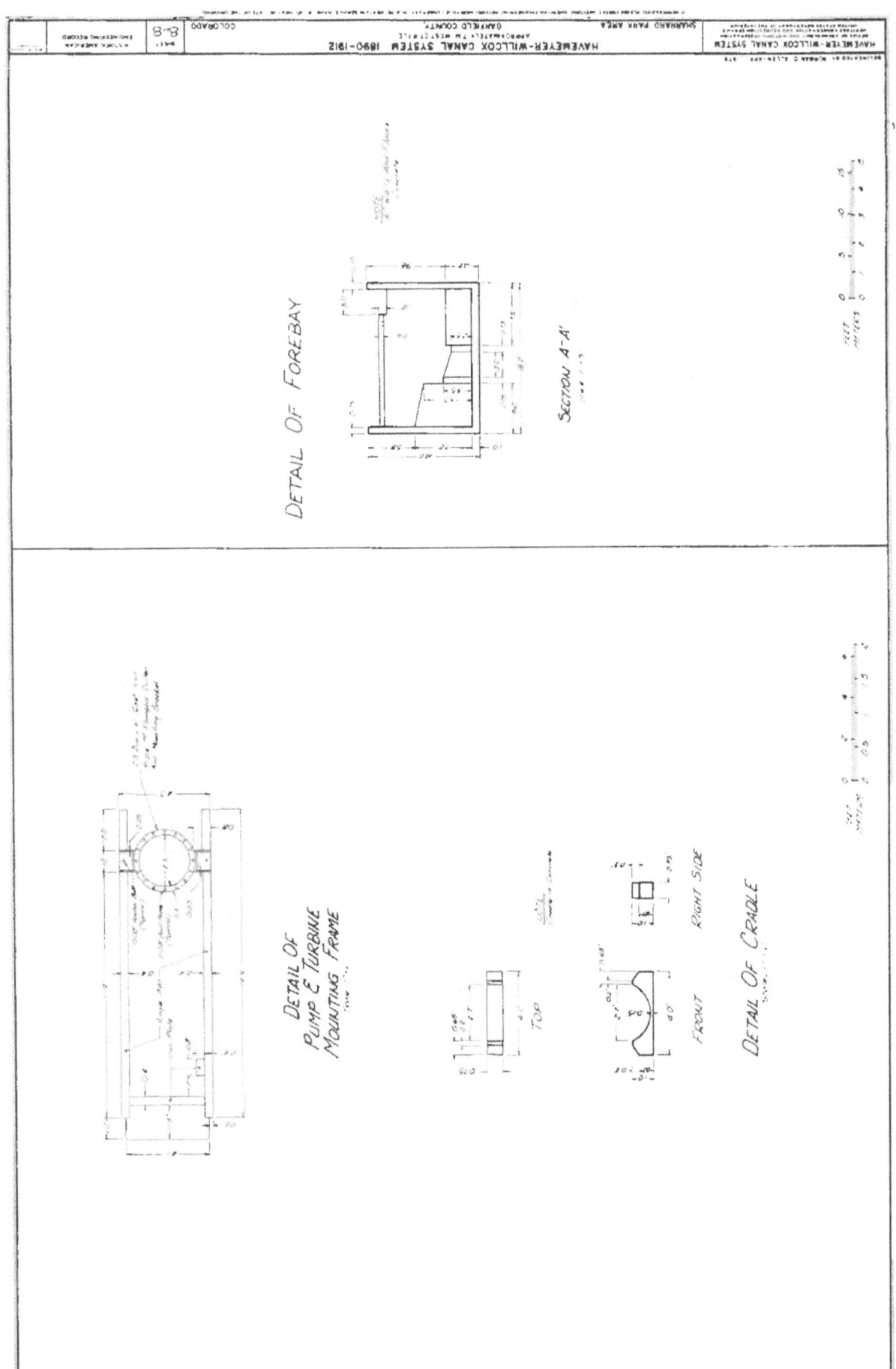

DETAIL OF FOREBAY

SECTION A-A'

DETAIL OF PUMP & TURBINE MOUNTING FRAME

TOP

FRONT   RIGHT SIDE

DETAIL OF CRADLE

Havemeyer-Willcox Canal System, Overview of Pumphouse and Forebay

Havemeyer-Willcox Canal System, Forebay Structure Facing West

Havemeyer-Willcox Canal System, Pumphouse Structure

Havemeyer–Willcox Canal System, Forebay Structure Facing South

ABOUT THE AUTHOR

Frederic J. Athearn is a life-long Colorado resident who was educated at the University of Colorado (Boulder), St. Louis University, and the University of Texas at Austin, where he earned a Ph.D degree in Western American History. He taught at the University of Texas, and the University of Colorado prior to becoming State Historian for the Bureau of Land Management in 1975. He is the author of two award-winning regional histories, several monographs, a number of professional history and photography articles and dozens of book reviews.

Dr. Athearn currently serves at the Colorado State Office, BLM, as Cultural Resources Program Manager and State Historian. He also is the Paleontology Resources Program Manager and is the Areas of Critical Environmental Concern coordinator. His primary interests include environmental history, regional history, and archival preservation of historic properties using photographic methods. Dr. Athearn has directed Historic American Building Surveys, Historic American Engineering Records, and has done numerous Level II photo recordations. He also teaches photography classes. He specializes in architectural recordation, studio figure photography, and historic preservation documentation.

U S GOVERNMENT PRINT NG OFFICE 1990 - 833 019

www.ingramcontent.com/pod-product-compliance
Lightning Source LLC
Chambersburg PA
CBHW080305290526
45790CB00005B/1936